POLLUTION, POLITICS, AND FOREIGN
INVESTMENT IN TAIWAN

Studies of the East Asian Institute, Columbia University

THE EAST ASIAN INSTITUTE OF COLUMBIA UNIVERSITY

The East Asian Institute is Columbia University's center for research, publication, and teaching on modern East Asia. The Studies of the East Asian Institute were inaugurated in 1962 to bring to a wider public the results of significant new research on Japan, China, and Korea.

TAIWAN IN THE MODERN WORLD

POLLUTION, POLITICS, AND FOREIGN INVESTMENT IN TAIWAN: THE LUKANG REBELLION

JAMES REARDON-ANDERSON

An East Gate Book

M.E. Sharpe

Armonk, New York
London, England

An East Gate Book

Copyright © 1992 by M. E. Sharpe, Inc.

Available in the United Kingdom and Europe from M. E. Sharpe,
Publishers, 3 Henrietta Street, London WC2E 8LU.

Library of Congress Cataloging-in-Publication Data

Reardon-Anderson, James.
Pollution, politics, and foreign investment in Taiwan :
the Lukang rebellion / James Reardon-Anderson
p.   cm. — (Taiwan in the modern world)
"An East Gate Book"
Includes bibliographical references.
ISBN 0-87332-702-0
1. Titanium Dioxide industry—Social aspects—
Taiwan—Lu-kang chen—Case studies.
2. Factories—Location—Social aspects—
Taiwan—Lu-kang chen—Case studies.
3. Pollution—Taiwan—Lu-kang chen—Case studies.
4. E. I. du Pont de Nemours & Company.
I. Title. II. Series.
HD9660.T583R43   1992
338.4′766105122′0951249—dc20
92-29888
CIP

Printed in the United States of America

The paper used in this publication meets the minimum requirements of
American National Standard for Information Sciences—
Permanence of Paper for Printed Library Materials,
ANSI Z39.48–1984.

MV   10   9   8   7   6   5   4   3   2   1

To
Matthew M. Gardner, Jr.
and
Lyman P. Van Slyke

CONTENTS

PREFACE

"LUKANG is just a little part of Chang-hua County," the old woman in the vegetable market observed. "Why does DuPont have to build its factory here? We are a democratic country, so those big officials must listen to us. Just like in a family, the old folks must listen to the young folks and make adjustments. This is the only way to have peace and happiness."[1]

Why did DuPont have to build a factory in Lukang? Why did the people of this town on the west coast of central Taiwan find the prospect so disturbing? And why did the parties to this dispute—the multinational corporation, the residents of Lukang and its surrounding communities, and the government in Taipei—have such difficulty resolving their differences, so that they could enjoy "peace and happiness," as the old lady said? These are the questions that made this an interesting story to write and, I hope, to read.

The Lukang "rebellion" was a series of well-organized mass demonstrations in 1986 and early 1987, whose objective was to block construction by the DuPont Corporation of a titanium dioxide plant in the Chang-Pin Industrial Zone, located near Lukang. If this protest had been tried just a few years earlier, it undoubtedly

---

[1]Interview with Mrs. Li Chao-chih in Lukang, July 1986, cited in *T'ai-ta hsüeh-sheng Tu-pang shih-chien tiao-ch'a-t'uan tsung-ho pao-kao-shu*, 75.

would have been crushed by a powerful government determined to promote development at any cost. If it had occurred a few years later, it probably would have passed unnoticed. But it came just at the time when environmental consciousness in Taiwan had reached critical mass and as the government was introducing political reforms that gave unprecedented scope to new forms of civic action. In this atmosphere, a handful of determined, capable activists, bent on keeping a giant multinational corporation out of their "old home," focused the attention of the entire island on this sleepy provincial town, raised the national consciousness about threats to the natural environment, and challenged the rules that government officials and industrial leaders in Taiwan had come to take for granted. The Lukang rebellion was one of those small events with large consequences that make for interesting and significant history.

This study of the events in Lukang has been possible because the key participants, from cabinet officials and corporate executives to cab drivers and fishermen, agreed to talk. The written record—newspapers, magazines, accounts and analyses of various sorts—has been helpful. But it is the voices of the actors themselves that make the story worth telling. Some informants were self-serving, even misleading, save that through their selective memories they revealed deeper insights into the meaning and motivation behind their deeds. Only one person I approached declined to talk, a few asked to remain anonymous, but everyone who agreed to speak did so on tape, which allowed me to get help translating thick accents and difficult passages and transcribe the conversations verbatim. Except for minor changes to correct grammar or smooth out transitions, the views and quotations that follow are presented exactly as I received them.

In addition to my twenty-odd informants, whose names and identities appear in the bibliography, other friends and colleagues contributed to this study in various ways. Some have asked to remain anonymous, some I would probably forget to mention if I tried, so let me thank them all—unnamed, but not unappreciated. Except for two, who unknowingly helped make this study possible and have enriched my life and career in countless other ways. I first learned of the events in Lukang in the fall of 1988, while I was serving as acting director of the Inter-University Program for Chinese Language Studies in Taipei. Everyone who has been close to the Stanford Center, as it is commonly called, knows that its great success has been due largely to the efforts of its executive secretary, Professor Lyman Van Slyke of Stanford University. Without Van's friendship and trust I would not have been in Taiwan at that time—nor had the confidence to sneak out of the office, now and then, to visit Lukang and interview participants in this saga. Nor would I have gone to Taiwan on that occasion without the support of another friend and colleague, Matthew Gardner, director of Asian Studies at Georgetown University, whom I had the pleasure of serving during my tenure as Sun Yat-sen Research Professor of Chinese Studies at Georgetown from 1985 to 1990. Matt has made a career of investing in others, and I am among the beneficiaries of his largesse. It is a pleasure to dedicate this book to these two gentlemen, as a small tribute to the contribution they have made to the study of Taiwan and relations between Taiwan and the United States.

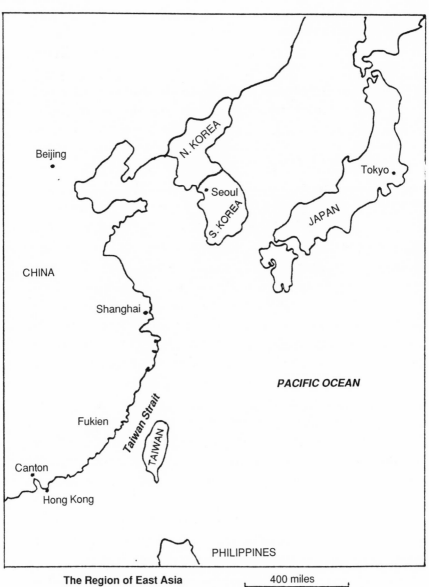

Beijing

CHINA

N. KOREA

Seoul
S. KOREA

Tokyo

JAPAN

Shanghai

PACIFIC OCEAN

Fukien

Taiwan Strait

TAIWAN

Canton

Hong Kong

PHILIPPINES

The Region of East Asia

|———— 400 miles ————|

POLLUTION, POLITICS, AND FOREIGN
INVESTMENT IN TAIWAN

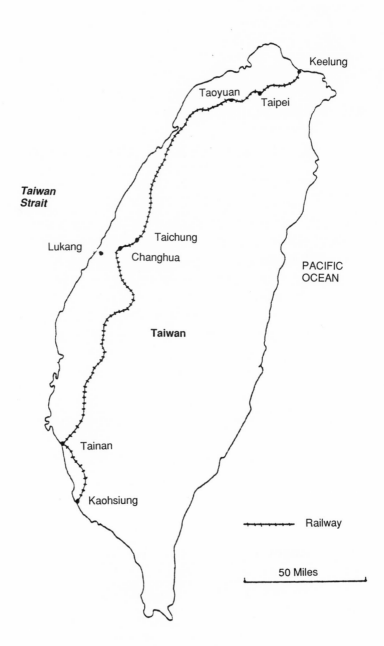

Keelung

Taoyuan
Taipei

Taiwan
Strait

Taichung
Lukang
Changhua

PACIFIC
OCEAN

Taiwan

Tainan

Kaohsiung

+++++++ Railway

50 Miles

THE LUKANG REBELLION

AT THE END of 1985, DuPont Taiwan Ltd., a wholly owned subsidiary of the American chemical giant, received permission from the government of the Republic of China (ROC) to build a titanium dioxide plant near the city of Lukang on the west coast of central Taiwan. For the next fifteen months, local activists mobilized the people of Lukang and the surrounding communities against a factory that they feared would destroy their environment and, by extension, their way of life. After a late start, the corporation fought back. Meanwhile, the government in Taipei, while supporting the project, struggled to balance its interest in economic development with the need for political stability. The clash among these forces sent seismic waves through Taiwan's society and politics, revealing the faults and fissures that lie beneath a normally opaque surface.

The Decision to Build

The agreement to locate a titanium dioxide plant in Taiwan and selection of the site near Lukang followed standard business considerations and established procedures on the part of both the ROC government and DuPont. DuPont wanted to manufacture titanium dioxide in Taiwan because sales of this chemical in the Far

3

East were brisk, and moving production facilities nearer the market would lower costs. By the mid-1980s, Taiwan was importing 30,000–40,000 tons per year of titanium dioxide, a white pigment used in paints, paper, plastics, and a variety of other products in Taiwan's booming petrochemical industry, most of it from DuPont plants in the United States. The factory envisioned for Taiwan would begin with a capacity of approximately the same amount and eventually double in size, with the surplus to be exported to Southeast Asia. DuPont hoped to build a similar facility in Korea. Together, the plants in Taiwan and Korea would make most of the titanium dioxide DuPont could sell in the Far East.[1]

Political considerations also influenced the decision. DuPont holds patents on the manufacture of titanium dioxide by the state-of-the-art "chlorine method." Taiwan, which permits foreign investors to come in on a wholly owned basis, offered protection for this proprietary technology. "Plus," one source inside the company confided, "the history of Taiwan had been that if you got the support of the central government, things would happen quickly, and we could be fairly confident that we could build in a timely fashion."[2] This expectation—that a deal struck with authorities in Taipei would hold throughout the island—was shared by government and

---

[1]"Tu-pang tsung-ching-li K'o-ssu-lu: kou-t'ung man-le i-pu" (DuPont general manager Costello: Communications one step late), *T'ien-hsia* 65 (October 1, 1986), 56; and interview with Mr. Kuo I-hsi of DuPont Taiwan, Ltd., *T'ai-ta hsüeh-sheng Tu-pang shih-chien tiao-ch'a-t'uan tsung-ho pao-kao-shu*, 82.

[2]Here and throughout, I have made use of information provided by persons familiar with DuPont Taiwan, Ltd., who have asked to remain anonymous. Subsequent mention of these sources will not be noted.

corporate officials and explains many of their later difficulties.

The calculations of ROC officials were primarily economic. Following the oil crisis of 1979, the Taiwan economy declined sharply, from double-digit growth in the 1970s to less than 4 percent in 1982. After rebounding in 1984, the growth rate dipped again during the first half of 1985. Even more troubling was the decline in investment, which fell from nearly 30 percent of GNP in 1980 to less than 20 percent during the first half of 1985, while imports of capital equipment and fixed domestic capital formation dropped to below the levels achieved the previous year. New capital from a high-profile multinational corporation would send a positive signal to investors at home and abroad who were waiting for signs that the recession was bottoming out. "In 1984, there was a short recovery," then Minister of Economic Affairs Li Ta-hai later explained, "but in the beginning of 1985, it turned bad again. Under these conditions, the government wanted to have new investment, which would in turn help boost the overall economy. This was the reason that the DuPont application was approved." DuPont's application, submitted on August 1, sailed through the Ministry of Economic Affairs (MOEA) in just eighteen days. The announcement was made at a joint press conference, designed to give maximum publicity to the $160 million deal, which was the largest single foreign investment in Taiwan's history and the largest by DuPont in the entire Far East.[3]

At this point, there had been no formal consideration

---

[3]Economic statistics: See sections on Taiwan in January-February issues of *Asian Survey* and *Asia Yearbook* for corresponding years. Quotation: interview with Li Ta-hai. Press conference: interview with David Liu.

of the impact a titanium dioxide plant might have on Taiwan's environment. Taiwan had no law requiring an environmental impact study prior to construction of a factory, by Chinese or foreigners. The ROC Environmental Protection Bureau (EPB), whose lowly rank within the Public Health Administration reflected the place this issue occupied on the nation's agenda, was not even informed that the DuPont case was under consideration. EPB head Chuang Chin-yüan learned of the decision by reading about it in the newspaper. Wang Chih-kang, executive secretary of the MOEA's Investment Evaluation Committee, which approved the project, explained why it was unfeasible to consult the EPB:

> Essentially, it is because environmental protection is a very complicated affair, and to decide whether or not [a particular plant] will create pollution, you must collect a great many environmental data and send them to the Environmental Protection Bureau, so that an evaluation might take a year and a half. This would cause the investment to lose its real effect. We are often criticized because our application procedures are complicated. If we had to go through an assessment by the EPB first, wouldn't this make it even more complicated?

ROC officials later defended the decision on the grounds that they knew and trusted DuPont, which had an outstanding reputation for safety in Taiwan and around the world. In fact, they argued, DuPont was favored over a domestic rival, Formosa Plastics, because the former had experience with the manufacture of titanium dioxide and an unblemished record in this field. To the end, these officials insisted that the DuPont project was safe and clean and, judged on its merits alone, deserved to be built.[4]

Selection of the site for the plant was made at the end of the year, again following standard business considerations. DuPont executives studied several sites owned by the government and available for purchase by enterprises that met the criteria for each area or zone. They eventually chose a plot in the Chang-pin Industrial Zone (CPIZ), because it was a large piece of land (over 500 hectares), a safe distance (3–5 km) from the nearest city (Lukang), yet near a large volume of water, port, and other transportation facilities, with suitable climatic conditions, access to customers and to areas where DuPont's expatriate employees would live, and, most of all, because the price was right. The Chang-pin site was one of several introduced to DuPont by the Ministry of Economic Affairs, which was responsible for developing and marketing the zone. It never occurred to company officials to ask whether the natives were friendly.[5]

The ministry may have been more anxious to sell property in the Chang-pin Zone than DuPont or other outsiders realized. Construction of the zone, a massive landfill off the coast of Chang-hua County, began in 1979 as part of a plan to bring more industry, particularly petrochemicals, to the center of the island, which had lagged behind the magnets of development in the north and south. The work, which was assigned to the

---

[4]Quotation: Lin Mei-no, "Wang Chih-kang cheng ho-chuan ch'eng-hsü wu-pu-t'o" (Wang Chih-kang declares there is nothing wrong with the approval procedures), *Tzu-li wan-pao*, August 26, 1986, 3. Other details: interviews with Chuang Chin-yüan, Hsü Kuo-an, and Li Ta-hai.

[5]The full title of the zone is the Chang-hua Coastal Industrial Zone (Chang-hua Pin-hai Kung-yeh Ch'ü). DuPont's selection of CPIZ: "Tu-pang tsung-ching-li K'o-ssu-lu," 57–58; and *T'ai-ta hsüeh-sheng Tu-pang shih-chien tiao-ch'a-t'uan tsung-ho pao-kao-shu*, 82.

The Chang-pin Industrial Zone. In 1986, the Chang-pin Industrial Zone was a massive, empty landfill off the west coast of central Taiwan, used only by squatters who laid their oyster lines along its embankments and weekend sunbathers who came to escape the summer heat. (Photo by James Reardon-Anderson)

Retired Servicemen's Engineering Agency, dragged on amid charges of corruption and mismanagement, while the general economic decline made it doubtful that a suitable buyer could be found. Finally, in late 1981, after NT $6.4 billion (U.S. $160 million) had been spent and only 500 of a planned 6,600 hectares completed, construction was halted. An irate President Chiang Ching-kuo denounced this waste of public money on a still-barren landfill. When they received DuPont's offer to buy this property, MOEA officials must have heaved a collective sigh of relief. The decision was announced in December: the people of Lukang were to have new neighbors.[6]

Sources of the Rebellion

Other than its size, there was little to distinguish the DuPont titanium dioxide project from similar undertakings elsewhere in Taiwan or to suggest that this case would prove incendiary. On the contrary, government and corporation officials expected only the problems normally associated with starting up a new enterprise, albeit one of some magnitude. Nor were they entirely at fault for failing to foresee the future, for the question of why the explosion occurred at this time and place is a complicated one. I begin by examining two elements of the fulminating compound: the rise of environmental consciousness in Taiwan, and the special character of Lukang and the surrounding communities.

Environmental Consciousness

By the mid-1980s, a growing number of people in all parts of Taiwan were uneasy, sometimes angry about the effects of pollution on the land Portuguese sailors had named Ilha Formosa, the "Beautiful Island." This environmental consciousness was fed in some cases by

---

[6] History of CPIZ: Lin Mei-no, "Tu-pang lai-te pu-shih shih-hou!" (It is not time for DuPont to come!), *Tzu-li wan-pao*, July 7, 1986, 3; and Lin Mei-no, "Wu Hui-jan t'ui-k'ai 'Chang-pin meng-yeh'" (Wu Hui-jan pushes aside "Chang-pin nightmares"), *Tzu-li wan-pao*, August 28, 1986, 3. The Retired Servicemen's Engineering Agency (Jung-min Kung-ch'eng-ch'u) is a unit of the Vocational Assistance Commission for Retired Servicemen (T'ui-ch'u I-kuan-ping Fu-tao Wei-yüan-hui) under the Executive Yuan. Chiang Ching-kuo: *Jen-chien* 10 (August 2, 1986), 37.

direct experience and everywhere by press reports of industrial pollution in Taiwan and abroad. For those who lived in Chang-hua County the chief culprit was the Taiwan Chemical Factory, a subsidiary of the petro-chemical giant Formosa Plastics, located in the county seat of Changhua. Ask a native of Changhua to tell you about his hometown and he might grip his nose between thumb and forefinger, mimicking a reaction to the stench that was the trademark of this city for two decades. In 1967, Taiwan Chemical was welcomed to Changhua with drums, parades, and dragon dances, for it promised to bring jobs and opportunities to the depressed center of the island. Soon, however, noxious gases filled the air, while employees who experienced health problems were reportedly denied proper treat-ment and compensation. Complaints against the fac-tory went unheeded. Chao Yao-tung, then chairman of the cabinet-level Council for Economic Planning and Development (CEPD), recognized the protest against DuPont as a "natural reaction" on the part of people who had put up for too long with the ill effects of the Changhua plant. "If you and I lived over there," Chao remarked, "definitely, emotionally, finally, we would not want any chemical plant in our area, because we suffered so much. This is the basic reason" for the opposition to DuPont.[7]

While the Changhua complex was mostly a nuisance, other chemical factories in Taiwan created more serious problems and provoked more determined opposition. In 1981, the peasants of Hua-t'an Village in Chang-hua County brought suit against local brick manufacturers, whose emissions had damaged neighboring rice paddies. This was the first collective antipollution suit presented

---

[7] Interview with Chao Yao-tung.

to a Taiwan court, and it resulted in an award of NT $1.5 million (U.S. $375,000) in damages. In 1983, residents of Lin-yüan, near Kaohsiung in southern Taiwan, burned down an amino acid factory that had been polluting the air and water of their village, forcing the factory to move to another site. In 1985, threats of violence against pesticide plants in Hsin-chu and T'ai-chung counties led the management of both factories to agree to clean up their operations. These so-called self-salvation (tzu-li chiu-chi) actions were initiated by local residents, usually poor farmers and fishermen, who had suffered damages, demanded compensation, and acted alone, using the means at hand, without the benefit of allies or support groups in other parts of the island.[8]

At the same time, another type of environmental movement, aimed at protecting such natural resources as the migratory birds of southern Taiwan and the mangrove forests of the north, was also gaining ground. Efforts of this sort pitted "enlightened" scholars and intellectuals from Taipei and other major cities against the poorer, less-educated hunters and woodsmen who were killing the birds or cutting the trees. In contrast to the sporadic, sometimes violent outbursts of aggrieved farmers and fishermen, the conservationists relied on sophisticated methods of influencing policy, worked through a network of professional colleagues around the island, and demanded not personal compensation but changes for the "common good." Both currents—the populist "self-salvation" and elitist conservationism—were amply reported in the press and known to the attentive public throughout Taiwan.[9]

---

[8]Hsiao Hsin-huang, Wo-men chih yu i-ke T'ai-wan, 191–93, 213–20.

News from outside Taiwan also helped shape perceptions of environmental hazards. Most dramatic, well
known, and damaging to DuPont was the tragedy of
Bhopal, India. In December 1984, leaks of poisonous
gas from the Union Carbide factory in Bhopal led to the
deaths of more than two thousand people, the largest
industrial accident in history. People throughout central Taiwan knew about Bhopal and that it had been
caused by an American chemical company—whether
Union Carbide or some other was for many a matter of
little importance. Celebrated cases of industrial pollution in Japan and elsewhere contributed further to the
perception that chemical factories, particularly foreign-
owned factories, were dangerous and out of control.[10]

Finally, two incidents in the spring of 1985 hit the
pocketbooks of almost everyone who made a living
along the coast of central Taiwan. In March, the
"green oyster" affair—the poisoning of shellfish in
southern Taiwan by emission of copper sulfate into
the sea—caused the price of oysters from all parts of
the island to fall by more than 60 percent. Just a few
months earlier, the poisoning of another shellfish in
eastern Taiwan had caused an even more precipitous
decline in prices. Although neither event affected the
size or quality of the Chang-hua oyster catch, both
caused substantial losses to oystermen throughout
Taiwan. More than 90 percent of the shellfish raised

---

[9]Ibid.

[10]Several accounts of these events mention the importance of
Bhopal in raising suspicions against DuPont. National Assemblyman and Lukang native Hsü Chih-k'un, who was inclined to
favor the DuPont project, felt that the example of Bhopal and the
possibility, however slight, that this tragedy might be repeated in
Taiwan effectively silenced him and other would-be supporters.
Interview with Hsü Chih-k'un.

in the Lukang region were exported to Japan. "The Japanese shellfish market is sensitive to industrial pollution," noted Ch'en Ching-hsiang, head of the Chang-hua County Fishermen's Association. "As soon as they find out there is a chemical factory in our fields, the market for our shellfish will collapse. If Du-Pont should come here, this will be big international news, and the Japanese will surely know about it." When word reached these maritime communities that DuPont planned to manufacture some strange new chemical and dump the waste offshore, most fishermen, oystermen, and shrimp and eel raisers were quick to join the opposition.[11]

These events and others like them raised fears in Taiwan about environmental pollution and lowered faith in the government's ability to control it. One public opinion poll showed that between 1983 and 1986, pollution moved from sixth to second most serious on a list of eight social problems, and from fourth to first among problems respondents expected to grow still worse in the future. Many people in Taiwan undoubtedly agreed with Hsü Han-ch'ing, a teacher in the Lukang Middle School, that the balance between the positive and negative effects of development had begun to tilt in the wrong direction. "At first, economic development covered only our ankles, and we wanted more," Hsü explained. "Now, it is up to our waists, and many people feel they have enough. What we fear most is that we'll find ourselves up to our necks in development, and then it will be too late."[12]

---

[11]Chung Ch'iao, "Yung Lu-kang-jen ti yen-ching lai k'an" (Seeing through the eyes of the Lukang people), Jen-chien, August 2, 1986, 19.

[12]Public opinion polls: Hsiao Hsin-huang, Wo-men chih yu i-ke T'ai-wan, 25–27. Quotation: Interview with Hsü Han-ch'ing.

Character of Lukang

Lukang Township and Chang-hua County as a whole had enjoyed less development and suffered less pollution than many other parts of Taiwan. The rebellion did not occur where the pressure of environmental decay was greatest. Rather, at least part of the explanation for the events of 1986 seems to lie in the character of the Lukang community. Lukang is a special place, and "Lukang men" have special feelings about it. "First, Tainan; second, Lukang; third, Meng-chia [Taipei]" is their motto, which locates this city both spatially and temporally at the center of Taiwan's earlier history, when Lukang's port served as the main entrepôt in the middle of the island and a magnet for commerce, learning, and culture. Several of the great temples that rise above the skyline and bind together Lukang residents in ritual and ceremony date from the late 1700s, the city's golden age. At the beginning of the present century, the harbor, which was built on sandy coastal flats and enjoyed a dubious preeminence as the best of a bad lot of central Taiwan alternatives, was abandoned in favor of the railroad that ran inland, through the county seat of Changhua to the natural harbors at the northern and southern ends of the island. Today, the harbor is filled up, the city has retreated from the coast, and only the faint scent of the sea recalls Lukang's lost glory. For generations, young people have been leaving this tired backwater for Taipei, Kaohsiung, and other cities that have felt more strongly the pulse of the modern world.[13]

---

[13]For historical background on Lukang, see Donald Deglopper, "Social Structure in a Nineteenth-Century Taiwanese Port City," and "Lu-kang: A City and Its Trading System." Recent statistics show that both Chang-hua County and Lukang Township continue to experience an annual net out-migration equal

Those who have stayed behind have been caught in the reality and clung to the myth of a fading past. The reality can be seen in Lukang's economic and social patterns. The backbone of the Lukang economy is its handicraft industries, led by manufacturers of traditional wooden furniture, small shops that offer religious articles to tourists and pilgrims, and stores that supply farmers and fishermen from the surrounding villages. The city straddles a single main street of storefronts, flanked by back alleys that house the workshops of carpenters, basket-weavers, metal-workers, and the like. Lukang has no big businesses or branch offices of large corporations headquartered elsewhere. Still, the economy in this part of the island has done well enough: In 1986, the average household income in Chang-hua County was about the same as for Taiwan as a whole, while the unemployment rate, 0.9 percent, was less than half the national average. Except for the growth of boxy, poured-concrete factories and tenements that surround the city, Lukang remains a market town, craft and religious center, a small but tranquil pool, unperturbed by the raging tide of upbeat, industrial Taiwan.[14]

These physical and economic structures help support a society tightly bound within and somewhat removed from the world without. Lukang's merchants, craftsmen, and petty entrepreneurs are not sharply differentiated by

to about 1 percent of the total population. See *Chung-hua min-kuo ch'i-shih-ch'i-nien Chang-hua-hsien t'ung-chi yao-lan*, 22–23. Note: Here and throughout, I use the standard romanization, Chang-hua, for the county, and the modified, Changhua, for the county seat.

[14]Household incomes: *Chung-hua min-kuo ch'i-shih-ch'i-nien Chang-hua-hsien t'ung-chi yao-lan*, 252–53. Unemployment rates: ibid., 34–35; and *T'ai-Min ti-ch'ü jen-k'ou t'ung-chi, 1987*, 172–73, 198–99.

wealth or status. Housing patterns mix rich and poor, managers and workers. Members of these variegated neighborhoods join in ritual activities, such as the birthday of the local deity, while ceremonies sponsored by larger temples, like that devoted to the sea goddess Matsu, draw together residents from all parts of the city. In Lukang, notes one native son, everyone is "related" (t'ung) in some way—by blood, by common surname, as school classmates, fellow villagers, or through temple committees and religious rituals. "Around here," people say, "everyone knows everyone else, and when something has to be done they just get together and do it." Few newcomers have moved in to take the place of the city's many emigrants, and those who try find it hard to penetrate the web of established relations. In sum, the economy, spatial organization, public ceremonies, and demographic patterns of Lukang all serve to strengthen the ties among Lukang residents and separate them from the world outside.[15]

In truth, Lukang is less separate and distinct than some natives of the city would like to pretend. Taiwan is a tiny, crowded island, no part of which has escaped the economic and technological changes of recent times. The 77,000 people of Lukang Township (chen), which includes the city and surrounding communities, are jammed up against their neighbors, pelted with breaking news and changing fashions, and in many

---

[15]Native son: first interview with Nien Hsi-lin. "Around here": Donald Deglopper, "Religion and Ritual in Lukang," 55. This and two other articles by Deglopper describe Lukang social and economic structure in the late 1960s. See Donald Deglopper, "Artisan Work and Life in Taiwan" and "Doing Business in Lukang." Recent testimony of Lukang residents and my own experience in Lukang suggest that much of what Deglopper described for that period remains true today.

Lukang temple. Temples serving a variety of local folk gods are the focus of Lukang social life. Leaders of the anti-DuPont movement reached their followers through community networks centered in these temples. (Photo courtesy of *Hsiang-ch'ing* Magazine)

cases rich enough to send their sons and daughters abroad to school—and then to follow them there on vacation, or to settle. Yet these developments seem to have strengthened the myth of Lukang's special status, as though champions of this city hope to find its meaning, and theirs, in a bygone era. To hear the locals tell it, Lukang is the last bastion of Taiwanese culture, carrying the torch of traditional virtue into the cold, raw world of modernity, a center of learning and culture that has recently and somewhat unjustifiably fallen on hard times. True to their mission, or so they imagine it, the people of Lukang retain their sense of community, quality, and commitment to the values of the past. Inside Lukang, "everyone knows everyone else, and people get along," they say, while outside the city, the scholarly talent of Lukang's sons illuminates the firmament. It is said that Lukang has the highest percentage of university graduates and holders of higher degrees of any place in Taiwan—a "fact" that was reported to me by several Lukang residents, although the available data suggest that it is almost certainly untrue.[16] Shih Wen-ping, poet, art dealer, and keeper of Lukang lore, explains how his fellow townsmen cling to their special identity, even as the reality that sustains it is fading:

> Although the forms of cooperation are decreasing in number, and although rituals and ceremonies tend to become simpler and less costly, it is evident that the community still places much (emphasis) on the cooperative spirit and that it regards itself as a distinctive social unit. . . . Lukang people take some pride in pointing out that they have an especially strong community spirit, in contrast to many neighboring towns. Lukang desires solidarity because "solidarity is strength."[17]

Both myth and reality played important roles in the struggle against DuPont. The small merchants, craftsmen, and shopkeepers who dominate the local economy saw little profit in a factory that would employ few townsmen and feared that the disruption of tourism or harm to the fishing industry would devastate their trade. Lukang lacks big business and big businessmen,

---

[16]Official statistics for 1987 show that the percentage of population with bachelor's degrees in Chang-hua County (1.5 percent) was less than half that for Taiwan as a whole (3.2 percent), while the percentage with graduate degrees in Chang-hua (0.048 percent) was less than one-third that for Taiwan as a whole (0.15 percent). Although these statistics give no breakdown by township, it is unlikely that Lukang is significantly more productive than other parts of the county, much less the nation. See *Chung-hua min-kuo T'ai-Min ti-ch'ü jen-k'ou t'ung-chi yao-lan*, 114–15, 140–41.

[17]Quoted in Won Tai-sheng, "Environmental Awareness Stimulates Grass Roots Democracy," 66.

who can envision the economic development of central Taiwan and how this transformation might serve their interests. Once the threat of DuPont was identified, opponents were easily mobilized through community networks and interpersonal connections. "Everything was done on the spot, without much planning," noted Shih Wen-ping. "When we wanted to act, we could assemble a thousand people in half an hour."[18] Finally, the myth of Lukang's special character, the fear that the temples would be disfigured by noxious gases and the society corrupted by outside forces, energized the movement throughout. In the minds of many locals, Lukang was a special place, and they meant to keep it so.

Although the leaders of the rebellion came from the city, and many of their followers were city folk, the strongest support came from the maritime communities surrounding Lukang. The coast of Chang-hua County, including the area adjacent to the Chang-pin Industrial Zone, is home to fishermen who work the shallow waters of the Taiwan Straits, oystermen whose harvest grows on wire vineyards that stretch between wooden poles in knee-deep water along the shore, and raisers of shrimp, eels, and other seafood whose artificial ponds dot the flat inland plain. Individually, many maritime folk are poor, uneducated, and lacking in all of the resources that move and shake Taiwan. Collectively, they constitute a major social and economic force. In 1986, the Chang-hua County Fishermen's Association boasted twelve thousand members, representing a total fishing community of fifty thousand people, who accounted for an estimated NT $8 billion (U.S. $20 million) in annual production, 90 percent of

---

[18]Interview with Shih Wen-ping.

An oysterman and his field. The backbone of the Lukang rebellion was the fishing communities along the coast. Following the "green oyster affair," oystermen feared the effect of pollution on their markets. Those who were squatting on government property knew they would be removed once work on the Chang-pin Industrial Zone resumed. (Photo courtesy of *Hsiang-ch'ing* Magazine)

which was exported to Japan. (By comparison, the Du-Pont plant promised employment for only two to three hundred local workers and had a projected annual output worth NT $2.5 billion.)[19]

Many local oystermen had been compensated by the government for their rights to coastal areas at the time construction on the CPIZ began. Later, when work on the zone was halted, the oystermen returned. Now, if Dupont moved in, they would be forced to leave. Other fishermen, whose access to the sea and rights to ponds on the coastal flats were unquestioned, also feared the impact the plant might have on their livelihood. When DuPont's critics took

---

[19]Won Tai-sheng, "Environmental Awareness Stimulates Grass Roots Democracy," 48; and Hsü Che-yen and Hsieh Tung-hua, "Ta-k'ai ta-men, kuan-te-ch'i-lai ma?" (Once the door is open, can it be closed?), *Chung-kuo shih-pao*, June 22, 1986, 3.

their case to the fishing villages, they found these communities still reeling from the "green oyster" affair and prepared for the worst. "The papers say DuPont will employ two hundred," noted one oysterman. "If DuPont comes, the seacoast is polluted, the fishing industry collapses, and fifty thousand jobs are reduced to two hundred, then the rest of us will just lie on our oyster beds and starve!" In an opinion poll of Lukang and Changhua residents conducted by National Taiwan University students in July 1986, 86 percent of all fishermen were "strongly opposed" to the DuPont plant, the highest percentage recorded for any occupational group (see appendix). It was not difficult to persuade fishermen in the Lukang region that the plant posed a threat. They supplied the movement to block DuPont with much of its money and many of its most rabid supporters.[20]

While not everyone in Lukang supported this struggle, those who did not join remained on the sidelines, rather than defend the government and the corporation. Even the most highly placed Lukang natives, men who throughout their careers had backed the ruling party and its program to promote industrialization, refused to speak up for DuPont. Hsü Chih-k'un, one of two members of the National Assembly elected by the business constituency, stayed in close touch throughout this period with three other prominent Lukang residents: Minister of Justice Shih Ch'i-yang, Control Yuan Vice-president Hwang Tzuen-chiou (Huang Tsun-ch'iu), and Taiwan Cement Company President Ku Chen-fu. According to Hsü, all four men supported the strategy

---

[20]Role of fishermen: interview with Yeh Wan-ch'ung. Oysterman quotation: Chung Ch'iao, "Yung Lu-kang-jen ti yen-ching lai k'an," 22. Poll: *T'ai-ta hsüeh-sheng Tu-pang shih-chien tiao-ch'a-t'uan tsung-ho pao-kao-shu,* 55.

to expand industry in central Taiwan and had histori-
cally favored foreign investment of the type offered by
DuPont. But like everyone else who followed these
events, they were overwhelmed by the rapid-fire
charges against the proposed plant and confused by
the silence of the government and the corporation. "In
the beginning," Hsü recalled,

> I did not know what DuPont was doing. I asked an
> official at the Bureau of Industry, "What is DuPont going
> to make?" and he told me, "White powder (pai-fen)."
> "What is this white powder?" I asked. He did not know.
> If officials at the Bureau of Industry did not know what
> DuPont was up to, then a common merchant who had not
> even studied chemical engineering like myself could not
> possibly know. How could I explain this to the people?

DuPont's critics were raising questions, and no one was
giving the answers, while the tragedy of Bhopal, still
fresh in the public mind, silenced even the most bullish
proponents of change. "No one dared speak," recalled
Hsü Chih-k'un. "No one dared speak!"[21]

Finally, support for the DuPont project was made difficult because the movement to block the plant—unlike
previous protests in other parts of the island, which were
mounted by the victims of industrial pollution to demand
compensation for past damages—sought to prevent the
crime *before* it occurred. This made it easy for critics to
charge that the factory would produce some hypothetical
damage and hard for DuPont to prove it would not. And
since the factory had not been built, there were no DuPont
employees, suppliers, service industries, or others in the
community who could vouch for the plant's safety or,
because they benefited from association with the company, might come to its defense.

---

[21]Interview with Hsü Chih-k'un.

Leaders of the Rebellion

The rise of environmental consciousness in Taiwan and the special character of Lukang and its surrounding communities may have been important, even necessary, factors in the struggle against DuPont, but they were not sufficient to assure its success. For there was no established model or path by which these forces could be brought to bear on the problem, or even a clear conception of what that problem was. The crucial piece was leadership. It was leadership that set the "Lukang rebellion" apart from other environmental protests in Taiwan, before and since.

The creator and sustainer of the anti-DuPont movement, as it was dubbed in the press, was Lukang businessman, civic activist, and politician Li Tung-liang. Li describes himself as a "Lukang-man," and as he talks there is a hint of confusion about where the "Lukang" ends and the "man" begins. He was born, was raised, lives, and will probably die in Lukang, and no one is more anxious or able to speak of its virtues than he. A middle school dropout, Li served in the army and worked for a time in Taipei before returning home to take over the family store, which sells incense and other religious paraphernalia to the tourists, pilgrims, and curiosity-seekers who flock to Lukang's temples and festivals. At the time of the DuPont affair, he reportedly worked in the incense store, drove a small delivery truck, and lived in modest circumstances.[22]

---

[22]For information on Li's biography, see *Jen-chien*, August 2, 1986, 24–31; and interview with Li Tung-liang. Details on Li's personal circumstances were provided by Ch'en Chih-ch'eng, Lukang correspondent for *Chung-kuo shih-pao*, who by all accounts was a confidant of Li during the first half of 1986.

Li Tung-liang, forty-eight years old in 1986, cuts an impressive figure: Tall, stocky, handsome, hail-fellow well met, he greets everyone by name and is known to down six or seven bottles of rice wine in the late-night drinking parties that bond Taiwanese men and fuel their politics. Surprisingly, he combines this masculine shape with a twinkling, childlike manner that lends credibility to his often simple, even naïve statements about himself and his hometown. In a society where neighborly familiarity is prized, male comaraderie cherished, and glib statements about lofty virtue and local honor ring true, Li Tung-liang has charisma to burn.

During the 1970s, Li won a reputation for reviving the luster of Lukang and putting the city back in the nation's consciousness. While serving as president of the local Junior Chamber of Commerce, he organized the Lukang National Folk Arts Festival, raised money from Lukang residents who had left home to make their fortunes in Taipei, and persuaded one of the television stations to broadcast several hours of this affair throughout the island. The festival was a great success: reminding the nation of Lukang's past glories and present charms, attracting scads of tourists, enriching the local economy, and filling Lukang people with pride. Li's reputation as a worthy native son was his greatest asset in the battle against DuPont, as one old woman, interviewed in the Lukang vegetable market at the height of the struggle, explained.

> Li is a nice young guy. In the (National Folk Arts) Festival, he successfully boosted Lukang's image and restored Lukang people's dignity. We were proud of gaining face in this national event. Now, he again leads the anti-DuPont movement, trying to prevent our cultural heritage from outsiders' intrusions. I don't really know

what is the real argument of the DuPont titanium dioxide plant, but I know this guy, so why shouldn't we
Lukang people support him?[23]

By all accounts, Li was the first person in Lukang to
recognize the significance of a short article that appeared
in the Taipei press in December 1985 announcing the
decision to sell a piece of the Chang-pin Industrial Zone
to DuPont for construction of a titanium dioxide plant.
Until then, neither corporate nor government officials
had offered to discuss these plans with residents of the
area. Even Chang-hua County Magistrate Huang Shih-
ch'eng learned of the decision by reading about it in the
newspaper. There was nothing unusual in this. The
government owns the industrial zones and has authority to dispose of their assets. Major economic policies
had always been made in Taipei, and government officials, most of whom belonged to the ruling Kuomintang
party, were not in the habit of consulting members of
the "nonparty" (tang-wai) opposition, like magistrate
Huang. Everyone involved in the decision later testified
that they expected no problems in Lukang and treated
the move like any other. What was special about this
case was that a few people in the area most affected
were sufficiently alarmed by the news to try to do something about it.[24]

At first, neither Li Tung-liang nor anyone else in
Lukang had the slightest idea what titanium dioxide
was or how its manufacture might affect their locale,
but they held deep suspicions about chemical industries, the ability of the government to control them, and

---

[23]Won Tai-sheng, "Environmental Awareness Stimulates
Grass Roots Democracy," 77.
[24]Interview with Huang Shih-ch'eng.

their potential for doing harm. As he looked into the problem, Li discovered that titanium dioxide is a non-toxic, noncombustible, apparently harmless substance, and that the chlorine method, which DuPont planned to use, was safer and less polluting than the older sulfuric acid method employed by Japanese factories in other parts of Taiwan. Still, questions about the potential side effects remained unanswered. Large amounts of liquid chlorine would have to be stored at the Changpin site, and a leak in the storage tanks could spread toxic gases to nearby Lukang. Equally troubling was the wastewater: hot and highly concentrated with ferric chloride, a toxic substance that could threaten the well-being of marine life along the coast. Given Taiwan's record of gross negligence in dealing with industrial pollution and environmental hazards, there was ample cause for concern.[25]

It was not so obvious, however, how opponents of the factory should proceed. There was no precedent in Taiwan for attempting to block a construction project, particularly one of this magnitude, on environmental or any other grounds. The system offered no channel for judicial or administrative review, and there was no organization, strategy, or experience on which proponents of civic action might draw. Li Tung-liang claims that at the outset he and the other leaders of this movement were driven by a simple motive—to save Lukang—and had no master plan. Looking back, he describes the movement with a disarming naïveté that, calculated or sincere, always found a ready audience:

> In the beginning, we had no strategy. We had only our determination. We were country folk, and we did not want a chemical factory in our neighborhood. I knew

---

[25]*T'ien-hsia* 65 (October 1, 1986), 56–57.

this was difficult, but I had confidence. The Chinese have a saying: "When you act with wholehearted dedication, even the stones will part to let you by." In this instance, I acted with complete honesty and without concern for myself. I did it for the common good. I did not want my hometown polluted. That was the starting point. I thought, "If our starting point is right and proper, if we are not striving for power or seeking private interests, if we are honestly doing the right thing, then we will win the support of people throughout the country and especially the scholarly community." That was what I was thinking. In the beginning, we had no plan.[26]

Yet there was a plan of sorts. Li began by collecting signatures on a petition opposing construction of the plant. This practice, known as *ch'en-ch'ing*, was commonly employed in Taiwan, as it had been in late imperial China, to communicate popular opinion to government authorities. Li had promised to lead such a petition drive in the course of his campaign for election to the Chang-hua County Assembly in January. Although he won his seat with the largest number of votes in the county, most observers agree that this was due less to his opposition to DuPont, an issue that was still not widely recognized, than to his previous record as champion of Lukang causes. Still, after the election, Li moved immediately to fulfill his campaign pledge, and within a month collected some sixteen thousand signatures. Why did so many people sign? Li credits his personal influence more than the public's understanding of the issues:

My record as chairman of various organizations had a great impression on the people of my hometown. Everyone

---

[26]Interview with Li Tung-liang. Chinese saying: "Ching-ch'eng so-chih, chin-shih wei-k'ai."

Li Tung-liang petitions against DuPont. At first, Li recruited supporters face to face, one by one. Many who signed the petition did so
more on the basis of personal trust than an understanding of the issues. (Photo courtesy of Niu-tun Publishing Company)

> knew that I had made sacrifices and contributions. I
> love my home and I spoke honestly. When I went out
> and asked for signatures, I talked to one, two people at
> a time and tried to make them understand. They really
> did not understand very much, but they trusted me.
> Many people signed.[27]

Li recognized that this initial response, which came
easily and mostly on faith, would not sustain the movement for long. To increase public awareness and attract
support, he moved next to sponsor a series of lectures
and slide shows that presented the case against Du-
Pont to town meetings and informal gatherings up and

---

[27]*Ch'en-ch'ing:* first interview with Nien Hsi-lin. Quotation:
interview with Li Tung-liang.

down the Chang-hua coast, particularly in the maritime communities that had most to lose if the Chang-pin Industrial Zone was developed. The information supplied in these meetings may have been factual, but much of it had nothing to do with titanium dioxide or problems posed by the DuPont plant. The presentations were critical of the corporation and the government and in some cases—for example, the colored slides showing victims of deadly and painful mercury- or cadmium-poisoning—inflammatory and misleading. Fair or unfair, these programs persuaded fishermen, oystermen, and raisers of shrimp and eels to see DuPont as a threat to their fragile livelihood. In Lukang itself, primary and middle school students were recruited to paint posters warning of the dangers of environmental pollution, which were displayed along the main street during the Folk Arts Festival in June, when the city was jammed with tourists, reporters, and television crews.[28]

Although Li Tung-liang tends to recall the defense of Lukang as his personal crusade, he was not alone. Li's chief collaborator was a former classmate and retired schoolteacher, Nien Hsi-lin, who managed Li's election campaign and served as his secretary during the year-long anti-DuPont movement. One of eight sons from a farming family outside of Lukang who had squeezed his way between rural poverty and educational ambition, short, squat, crude in appearance, but clear in thought and direct in speech, Nien provided the intellect and realism needed to complement Li's spacy charisma. Insiders remember Nien as the real brains of the movement. The man who represented DuPont in talks with the rebels recalls that Nien was well informed

---

[28]First interview with Nien Hsi-lin.

Nien Hsi-lin makes the case against DuPont. Open-air lectures and public forums like this one, held in front of Lukang's main temple, alerted residents to the threat of the chemical factory. (Photo courtesy of *Jen-chien* Magazine)

on the issues and asked most of the questions, while Li listened. It was widely rumored that Nien had been forced to resign his teaching position when he was caught in a scandal involving the showing of pornographic films, and that he went to work for Li in part because he needed the job. After the struggle with DuPont ended, Nien left town in apparent disgrace. Yet Nien Hsi-lin maintained greater respect for Li Tung-liang and other members of the movement than he received in return, and his analysis of what transpired in Lukang is consistently more insightful and less self-serving than that of any of his detractors.

Alone among the Lukang activists, he remains a force in Taiwan's environmental affairs.[29]

Li Tung-liang and Nien Hsi-lin took the first steps—to investigate the problem, launch the petition drive, organize the lectures and posters. Later, as their activities expanded, so did their need for assistance, and others were drawn in. Shih Wen-ping, a man of letters and chairman of the local cultural society, whose teeth are stained alternately red and yellow from betel-nut and Long Life cigarettes, which he chews and smokes at the same time, wrote propaganda pieces, gave interviews to the press, and provided the movement with intellectual respectability. Ch'en Ching-hsiang, head of the Chang-hua Fishermen's Association, helped bring his organization, which up until that time had been loyal to the Kuomintang, in on the side of the protesters. These and other friends of long standing began to meet informally, discuss strategy, and contribute, financially or in kind, when needed. As their expenses mounted and the need to gain wider recognition and credibility became more deeply felt, they agreed to set up a legal entity that could accept contributions and give the movement a cachet of legitimacy.

On May 28, Li Tung-liang submitted an application to establish the Chang-hua County Nuisance Prevention Association (Chang-hua Hsien Kung-hai Fang-chih Hsieh-hui). This application, which had to be reviewed by the local security agencies and Kuomintang party branch, was not approved until October 12, although "preparatory meetings" were held in the interim. The association eventually attracted three hundred members,

---

[29]Details on Nien biography: second interview with Nien Hsi-lin. DuPont representative: interview with C. K. Chen. Scandal: interview with Ch'en Chih-ch'eng.

who reportedly contributed NT $1,000-$20,000 (U.S. $25-$500) apiece, sufficient to cover expenses during the first year. It was chaired by Li Tung-liang and governed by a board of directors, drawn from across the spectrum of Lukang civic organizations. These included the directors of the various labor associations—farmers, fishermen, woodcutters—heads of the pan-Lukang and neighborhood temple committees, leaders of the women's, youth, senior citizens', and cultural societies, and presidents of the Junior Chamber of Commerce and the Lions' Club. The association formally served as the governing body of the anti-Dupont movement, and various activities were undertaken in its name, although most of the key decisions were made and initiatives taken by Li, Nien, and a handful of insiders.[30]

Li Tung-liang and the other Lukang leaders gave this movement its special cast. These men (there were no women in the leadership and precious few among the rank and file) had not attended university, gone abroad to study, or sought careers outside their hometown. Their place was in Lukang. They had a well-developed, perhaps overdeveloped, sense of its importance, and they did not want to give it up to others. But they were also accomplished men of affairs who had seen something of the world and were determined to defend their turf by winning the recognition and respect of their peers in other parts of Taiwan. Men of Li's stature disdained the tactics of those poor farmers and fishermen who had taken to sabotaging factories in the name of "self-salvation." Rejecting violence, they followed a

_____

[30]For a list of organizations represented on the board of the NPA, see Won Tai-sheng, "Environmental Awareness Stimulates Grass Roots Democracy." Other details: interviews with Li Tung-liang and Nien Hsi-lin.

strategy designed to establish the legitimacy of their claim—if possible, with the government and ruling party; if not, then with scholars, intellectuals, and opinion makers in Taipei—and through a combination of reasoned arguments and broad public support to secure a favorable resolution of the dispute. To achieve this goal, they had to negotiate a narrow, meandering path, between violence that would discredit their efforts, on one side, and acquiescence that would surrender their goals, on the other. And they had to achieve this without the benefit of previous experience or examples from which to learn.

DuPont Meets Its Critics

Li Tung-liang brought his protest to Taipei on March 13, when he delivered copies of the petition to the Executive Yuan, the Legislative Yuan, and the Kuomintang party headquarters. That afternoon he planned to take his delegation to call on the offices of DuPont Taiwan. Warned that they were coming, DuPont President Paul Costello invited the visitors in. It was the first meeting between company executives and their critics from down-island.

Up to this time, DuPont had made no public statement about its plan to build a factory in the Chang-pin Industrial Zone. The company's policy was to withhold announcement of major construction projects until the funds had been authorized, so as not to raise expectations that might go unfulfilled. Until the beginning of March, DuPont Taiwan was waiting for the green light from corporate headquarters in Wilmington. Consistent with this approach, the established practice for foreign investors in Taiwan was to let Taipei handle public relations. DuPont was to be a tenant in a government-

DuPont Taiwan president, Paul Costello. Following corporate policy and ROC government advice, Costello at first kept silent on the proposed plant. Later, he admitted that this approach left public opinion at the mercy of DuPont's critics. (Photo courtesy of the DuPont Corporation)

owned industrial zone, and it made sense to let the landlord deal with the neighbors. ROC officials advised DuPont to keep a low profile, not to engage the Lukang community in open debate, and to follow Taipei's lead. DuPont, whose two existing Taiwan plants were in other parts of the island, lacked connections in Chang-hua County. The company had little choice but to take the government's advice.[31]

Still, DuPont executives were anxious to break the

---

[31]"Tu-pang tsung-ching-li K'o-ssu-lu," 57.

silence, open talks with local leaders, and get their message out. In early March, the parent company authorized funds for the Taiwan project, and a second corporate policy took effect: namely, to develop good relations with the surrounding community. DuPont spokesmen are quick to point out that this approach is a matter of simple necessity. In the late twentieth century, they argue, no community anywhere in the world wants a chemical factory next door. Acceptance must be earned by keeping a clean record, honest dealings, and effective public relations. Paul Costello later admitted that much valuable time had been lost while opposition to the plant mounted and the company remained silent. He had only twenty-four hours' notice of Li Tung-liang's visit, but he saw this as a chance to begin building bridges to DuPont's new neighbors.[32]

The two sides came away from the March 13 meeting with different readings of what had transpired. DuPont executives called the session "very positive." Chinese staff members briefed their visitors on the corporation, its work in Taiwan, and the manufacture of titanium dioxide. They thought they had established contacts that would help the company make its case to the Lukang community. It was a "good start" on the dialogue DuPont considered essential to doing business in Taiwan. It is clear from their later actions, however, that the visitors from Lukang did not see it that way. They returned home convinced that they would have to fight to protect their turf.

Whatever hopes DuPont may have had for a dialogue were dashed when Paul Costello visited Changhua in April to pay a courtesy call on County Magistrate

---

[32]Ibid.

Huang Shih-ch'eng and explain plans for building a factory in Huang's backyard. Costello arrived to find that Huang had invited Li Tung-liang and other Lukang residents and journalists to their meeting, which degenerated into what the DuPont executive later called a "painful" experience, marked by scurrilous charges against himself and his company. From this point on, DuPont remained convinced that the leaders of the protest were committed to blocking construction of the plant, that they were pursuing this goal by spreading what they knew to be false and damaging information, and that there was no way the corporation could dissuade them from this course.[33]

By late spring, DuPont officials saw the situation slipping out of control. If they did not stop the tide of adverse publicity, it would soon be too late to regain public confidence. They needed what one source called a "quick fix" to get back to "ground zero." One of DuPont's problems was that its two existing factories in Taiwan made products—electronic equipment and fertilizers—that were far removed from titanium dioxide. The company could invite journalists and community leaders to inspect these plants, which had won prizes for safety and cleanliness, and many visitors were favorably impressed. But DuPont had no titanium dioxide facility in Taiwan and no one on the local staff qualified to explain how this chemical was made, and made safely. The solution, or so the company and its supporters in the government hoped, was to invite influential figures from Lukang and Chang-hua County to visit and report back on titanium dioxide plants in the United States. The trip, which took place from June 5

---

[33]Lin Mei-no, "Tu-pang pu-hui ch'ing-yen fang-ch'i" (DuPont will not give up lightly), *Tzu-li wan-pao*, August 14, 1986, 3.

to June 20, was organized and led by Chuang Chin-yüan, head of the Environmental Protection Bureau, who later admitted that his object was to show these people the best side of DuPont's operations and "convince them that this was a good, safe investment for Taiwan."[34]

The delegation included several men who, if properly impressed, should have been in a position to persuade skeptics back home. Lukang Mayor Wang Fu-ju, Lukang City Council Speaker Yeh Wan-ch'ung, and Chang-hua County Assembly Deputy Speaker Hsieh Shih-ku had at first accepted the unrefuted charges against the company and joined the chorus of critics. Wang was in fact elected on a platform to support the petition against DuPont, although he did nothing to assist Li Tung-liang in that effort. Another member of the delegation, *Chung-kuo shih-pao* (China times) Lukang correspondent Ch'en Chih-ch'eng, was a confidant of Li Tung-liang and privately sympathized with his campaign against the factory. The government tried to persuade Li Tung-liang to join the delegation, and up until two days before the departure it was assumed that Li would go, but at the last minute he backed out, claiming that he lacked the expertise needed to make an informed judgment. Even some of his friends found that excuse hard to swallow. Ch'en Chih-ch'eng maintains that Li declined because he knew if he visited the factories, found that they did not cause serious pollution, and admitted the fact, "his supporters would accuse him of being bought off by DuPont" and his political career would be ruined. Li himself admitted, somewhat

---

[34]DuPont's problems: interviews with C. K. Chen and Ch'en Chih-ch'eng. Chuang Chin-yüan: interview with Chuang Chin-yüan.

cryptically, that he reversed his decision because the "fear of rumors" (jen-yen k'o-wei), which in this part of Taiwan might well point to charges of corruption.[35]

As supporters of the DuPont project hoped, the three local officials and one journalist who visited the titanium dioxide plants in the United States were turned completely around. All had left Taiwan believing that the charges against DuPont were true and that construction of the proposed factory would harm the environment. All reported that the titanium dioxide factories they visited were clean, apparently safe, and surrounded by attractive green spaces and quiet residential areas. All returned to Taiwan convinced that a similar plant should be built in the Chang-pin Industrial Zone. And—if Li Tung-liang needed any assurance that his decision to stay home was a wise one—all were greeted by withering criticism, including charges that they had been bought off by the government, the corporation, or both. Mayor Wang Fu-ju took the brunt of the criticism, having to fend off a recall campaign, but other members of the delegation were pilloried in public and threatened with hate mail and phone calls. The journalist, Ch'en Chih-ch'eng, saw his friendship with Li Tung-liang sour. "He did not like what I was saying," Ch'en explained.

> I began telling him that he should not put up such a fight, that he should listen to others and not keep up the street demonstrations. In my heart, I thought DuPont was right, although I did not say this openly in my articles. What I said was that people should not demonstrate in the streets, but should listen and try to understand. If DuPont could be persuaded to do the right

---

[35]Ch'en Chih-ch'eng: interview with Ch'en Chih-ch'eng. Li Tung-liang: interview with Li Tung-liang.

DuPont titanium dioxide plant in Edgemoor, Delaware. The delegation from Taiwan that visited DuPont factories in the U.S. found them to be safe and clean, but skeptics and committed foes of DuPont in Lukang never accepted these reports. (Photo courtesy of the DuPont Corporation)

thing, then we should accept the plant. But Li Tung-
liang did not want to hear this, so in the end he did not
like me.

Despite the testimony of local officials and the report
of the delegation, which supported construction of the
plant and gratuitously attacked the critics in Lukang,
the June trip did little to improve the reputation of
DuPont or the Chang-pin project. Opponents in Lukang
would not be persuaded; they sought to discredit the
findings of the delegation by charging that its members
had been duped or bribed or both.[36]

The Demonstration in Lukang

The turning point for the anti-DuPont movement came
on June 24, when several hundred Lukang residents
took to the streets, in defiance of martial law, to protest construction of the proposed plant. This demonstration, the largest in Taiwan since the Kaohsiung
"riot" of 1979, challenged not only the plan to locate a
chemical factory on the Chang-hua coast, but the very

---

[36]The identical version of these events was reported to me in
separate interviews by Wang Fu-ju, Yeh Wan-ch'ung, Hsieh
Shih-ku, and Ch'en Chih-ch'eng. Contemporary sources also
support this account: T'ai-ta hsüeh-sheng Tu-pang shih-chien
tiao-ch'a-t'uan tsung-ho pao-kao-shu, 113–14, 124; Chung-kuo
shih-pao, June 22, 1986, 3; and Lien-ho pao, June 28, 1986, 3.
Chang-hua County Assemblyman Chang Shun-ch'ang, after vis-
iting DuPont plants in the United States and stating his support
for construction of a titanium dioxide plant in Taiwan, received
hate mail and threatening phone calls. See Ch'i-shih nien-tai
fan-wu-jan tzu-li chiu-chi ti chieh-kou yü kuo-ch'eng fen-hsi, 92.
Ch'en Chih-ch'eng quotation: interview with Ch'en Chih-ch'eng.
Report of the delegation to the United States: Chuang Chin-yüan
et al., "K'ao-cha Mei-kuo Tu-pang kung-szu erh-yang-hua-t'ai
kung-ch'ang wu-jan k'ung-chih she-shih pao-kao-shu."

authority of the government to make and implement policy in this arena. The decision to risk civil disobedience shows that the Lukang leadership, while courting public opinion and the approval of the Taipei elite, felt desperate enough to cross the line of accepted behavior.

In early June, the preparatory committee that had been set up to direct the struggle against DuPont, pending approval of a formal association, sponsored a poster campaign for elementary and secondary students devoted to protecting the environment and combating industrial pollution. The Lukang Junior Chamber of Commerce supplied paint and brushes, the carpenters' union made 150 large posters, and more than 300 students contributed their art work. Although the announced theme of the campaign was purposely broad, many of the posters focused on the threat of titanium dioxide and the DuPont plant. When the Lukang Folk Arts Festival opened in the second half of June, the posters, some of which contained incendiary attacks on the proposed factory, were displayed along both sides of the main street.[37]

On the afternoon of June 23, word reached Lukang that the next day television crews would arrive to film the posters and other attractions of the festival. That evening, several people who had been active in the movement met at Li Tung-liang's home to talk about how they might take advantage of this event. The anti-DuPont activists, like their corporate counterparts, felt that time was running out. More than three months had passed since Li presented their petition in Taipei, and still they had received no reply. The people of

[37] *Ch'i-shih nien-tai fan-wu-jan tzu-li chiu-chi ti chieh-kou yü kuo-ch'eng fen-hsi*, 85.

Lukang school children painting antipollution posters. During the annual Folk Arts Festival in June, the streets of Lukang were lined with posters like this one, which calls for opposition to the DuPont plant whose noxious gases might threaten the health of local residents. Television crews that came to film this display were on hand for the June 24 demonstration. (Photo courtesy of *Jen-chien* Magazine)

Lukang and the surrounding villages had joined the opposition to DuPont, but word of their protest had not spread beyond the county. The leading dailies ignored the issue or buried it in the back pages among the "local news." Meanwhile, the government had begun preparations to widen the road through Lukang for construction of the DuPont plant. Work on the road was a particularly sore subject, because for years the Lukang City Council had been trying without success to get Taipei to improve this thoroughfare. Now it was to be done for the benefit of foreign investors, while local taxpayers would have to bear much of the cost. If something did not happen soon, the government would literally steamroller its way through Lukang.[38]

There was no shortage of hotheads in and around the city who offered to block construction of the plant by throwing themselves in the path of the oncoming trucks, but more sober minds had to weigh carefully the risks of open confrontation. Under martial law, which remained in effect until July 1987, assemblies of more than ten people required official approval, and there was no question of getting permission for a demonstration that openly challenged the government. People charged with inciting the Kaohsiung riot were still in jail. Leaders of the anti-DuPont movement deny that they feared for their personal safety and claim that their chief concern was that a demonstration or other act of civil disobedience might alienate the generally conservative public whose support they were trying to attract. If a demonstration led to bloodshed, if policemen or innocent bystanders were injured and the demonstrators were shown to be responsible, public opinion in Taiwan, which had generally favored law and order, could swing to the government side. Even if there was no violence, some people otherwise sympathetic to the movement would nonetheless be alienated.[39]

---

[38]Expected arrival of TV crews: Lu Ssu-yüeh, "Tsou-shang chieh-t'ou fan Tu-pang" (Taking to the streets to oppose Du-Pont), *Hsiang-ch'ing yüeh-k'an* (August 1986), 41. This was the official journal of the Chang-hua County Nuisance Prevention Association, published monthly from August 1986 to February 1987, after which it was discontinued. June 23 meeting: *Chung-kuo shih-pao*, June 25, 1986, 3. Plans to widen the road through Lukang: *Tzu-yu jih-pao*, June 4, 1986, 11; *Lien-ho pao*, June 27, 1986, 3; and *T'ai-ta hsüeh-sheng Tu-pang shih-chien tiao-ch'a-t'uan tsung-ho pao-kao-shu*, 109–10.

[39]In interviews, Li Tung-liang, Nien Hsi-lin, Ch'en Ching-hsiang, and Shih Wen-ping all said that at the time they were concerned that a public demonstration would alienate the generally

All these arguments were considered on the evening of June 23, when the men meeting at Li Tung-liang's home decided that whatever the risks, they would take to the streets. In later accounts, all were disarmingly frank about what they hoped to achieve—to put Lukang in the headlines. They felt their previous efforts had failed, that DuPont and the government were ready to begin construction, and that the only way to block the factory was to shock people outside Chang-hua, especially scholars and intellectuals in Taipei, who could focus attention on this issue and persuade the government to reverse its course. These were conservative men who recognized the conservative bias of the society around them but were willing to risk a radical departure from established norms to advance their essentially conservative strategy of winning the support of Taiwan's opinion makers.[40]

They also knew they had to act quickly to avoid detection by security units that would move to block any act of open dissent. The next morning, film crews would be in Lukang, and the anti-Dupont forces could get into the streets before the police had time to react. "I made the decision on my own," Li Tung-liang later explained with typical immodesty. According to Li's account, friends urged him to keep his plans secret, on the grounds that police informants were watching, and followed his directions knowing that he acted for the common good. Others at the June 23 meeting have a different recollection. Nien Hsi-lin, who understood better and was more honest about the promise and pitfalls

conservative ROC citizenry. This, more than fear for their own safety, seems to have been the chief argument against taking to the streets.

[40]Interviews with Li Tung-liang, Nien Hsi-lin, Ch'en Ching-hsiang, and Shih Wen-ping.

of the movement, described the process of decision making during this period as follows.

> The Taiwanese have a saying: "When there is a model, follow it. When there is no model, figure things out for yourself." Before the anti-Dupont movement, Taiwan had no true environmental movement. And we never knew how long this movement would last. So we went forward, one step at a time, raising the level of the protest just a bit with each step. At first we followed the established practice of petitioning the government. But we discovered that petitions were of no use. At the time, we were still under martial law; the Formosa [Kaohsiung] affair had occurred just a few years before, and most people were very sensitive about getting involved in politics. We were afraid that if we raised the intensity too sharply, we would drive people away and be suppressed by the government. So we followed a step-by-step approach. After each step, we would see how the authorities reacted and how much popular support we had attracted. We would hold a meeting to weigh the pros and cons of the last event and plan the next one. The whole year was like that, advancing one step at a time.[41]

After the decision was made, preparations for the demonstration continued throughout the night. The slogan "I Love Lukang, Don't Want Dupont" (*Wo-ai Lu-kang, pu-yao Tu-pang*) was printed on three hundred T-shirts, the last one completed just before dawn. Journalists in Taipei were called and told to be in Lukang the next morning. At 8:00 A.M., one visitor to Li Tung-liang's home found him still busy phoning supporters to tell them the plans.[42]

---

[41]Ibid.

[42]Accounts of the June 24 demonstration appear in *Tzu-li wan-pao*, June 24 and 25, 1986, 3; *Chung-kuo shih-pao*, June 25, 1986, 3; *Lien-ho pao*, June 25, 1986, 3. Journalists in Taipei: Ts'ai Ming-te, "'Fan Tu-pang' she-ying pi-chi" (Photographic notes on "anti-DuPont"), *Jen-chien* 10 (August 2, 1986), 56–57.

By 9:30, five hundred to one thousand demonstrators (estimates vary), wearing the specially printed T-shirts and carrying banners and posters, gathered in front of the Wen-wu Temple at the east end of town, where television crews were expected to begin filming. Lukang Chief of Police Tsou Ch'ao-hua urged Li Tung-liang to keep the crowd under control and in place. But at 10:50—after waiting for the film crews to arrive—Li began the march along the one-mile course down Chung-shan Road, the main street of Lukang, to the T'ien-hou Kung Matsu Temple. On the way, the protesters waved banners, shouted slogans, and urged onlookers to join the parade. "We raised the atmosphere to the point where it was almost ready to burst into violence," confided Nien Hsi-lin. "Then, after the TV crews shot their film, we took down our banners and posters and cleared out."[43]

The demonstration achieved its goal of attracting islandwide attention. Stories and pictures of the protest were carried on television that night and in the front pages of the newspapers during the days that followed. An editorial in one leading daily, Chung-kuo shih-pao, treated the protest sympathetically and blamed the government's long record of environmental neglect for this explosion of "pent-up bitterness." Scholars and intellectuals took up the issue in forums and seminars. Even the president of the Academia Sinica, Wu Ta-yu, sided with the protesters. "In view of the record of pollution to our rivers, streams, and aquatic life," wrote Wu, "we certainly cannot blame the people for losing confidence in the government." A delegation of students

---

[43]Quotation: first interview with Nien Hsi-lin. Other details: Tzu-li wan-pao, June 24, 1986, 3; Chung-kuo shih-pao, June 25, 1986, 3; Lien-ho pao, June 25, 1986, 3.

Li Tung-liang talks to police on the morning of June 24. Li had no permit to hold a public meeting, which was a violation of martial law, and police urged him to contain the crowd. (Photo courtesy of Niu-tun Publishing Company)

from National Taiwan University spent their summer vacation in Lukang, investigating the situation and lending their support to the protest. One popular journal, *Jen-chien* (Among the people), devoted a whole issue to the "DuPont Affair." This success in attracting support from students, scholars, and intellectuals in the capital distinguishes the Lukang protest from the sporadic outbursts of farmers and fishermen in other parts of Taiwan and testifies to the sophistication and efficacy of the Lukang leadership.[44]

While the headlines were generally favorable, evidence collected after June 24 shows that leaders of the movement

---

[44]Editorial: *Chung-kuo shih-pao*, June 26, 1986, 2. Wu Ta-yu: Wu Ta-yu, "Jen-min ti hsin-hsin" (Confidence of the people), *Min-sheng pao*, July 11, 1986, 3.

The June 24 demonstration. Li Tung-liang, right, leads the orderly but vocal march down the main street of Lukang to the Matsu Temple. (Photo courtesy of *Jen-chien* Magazine)

POLLUTION, POLITICS, AND INVESTMENT 49

had been right to fear that they might alienate public opinion, for many people otherwise sympathetic to environmental concerns did *not* approve of the tactics adopted by the protesters. Students from National Taiwan University, who interviewed 447 residents of the Lukang/Changhua area during the period July 1–18, found that opposition to the DuPont factory (90 percent) was much greater than approval of the June 24 demonstration (56 percent). A telephone poll of 318 residents of greater Taipei, conducted by *Lien-ho pao* (United daily news) in early July, points to a similar conclusion. This poll measured perceptions and preferences regarding the competing goals of economic development and environmental protection. The overwhelming majority of respondents judged environmental protection more important (31 percent) or ranked the two equal (55 percent), while only a small minority (8 percent) favored economic growth. A majority of the same sample thought the government placed greater emphasis on the economy (53 percent) and that it had done a poor job in the area of pollution control (62 percent). Only 37 percent believed Taipei would be able to enforce strict controls on the proposed DuPont plant. Still, when it came to the question of Lukang, some respondents otherwise sympathetic to the environmental cause were turned off—only 40 percent approved of the public demonstrations. (See appendix for details on both polls.)[45]

Separate interviews with two Lukang middle school teachers, Hsü Han-ch'ing and Wang K'ang-shou, give a sense of the thinking of those who grew disillusioned with the anti-DuPont movement as it moved into the streets.

---

[45]NTU student survey: *T'ai-ta hsüeh-sheng Tu-pang shih-chien tiao-ch'a-t'uan tsung-ho pao-kao-shu*, 38, 41. *United Daily News* poll: *Lien-ho pao*, July 7, 1986, 3.

Strongly opposed to the spread of industrial pollution, Hsü
had signed Li Tung-liang's original petition and helped him
organize the June poster campaign. But when Li took his
protest to the streets, Hsü refused to follow. Hsü considered Li and his fellowtravelers "politicians" who were trying
to whip up support for themselves, while their followers
were mostly "lower elements, people without anything to
do, who had received some sort of payoff." Hsü, and the
"better-educated elements" of Lukang with whom he identified, disapproved of marches and demonstrations, which
he thought also constituted "a form of pollution or harm
to society as a whole." Wang K'ang-shou drew a similar
distinction between the rabble who followed Li Tung-liang
and the educated elite, like himself, who maintained a
proper reserve. When asked if other teachers had taken
part in the marches, Wang laughed: "No, the intellectual
class shunned this movement and refused to join the
demonstrations."[46]

The survey conducted by NTU students in Lukang
and Changhua in early July shows that the prevalence
and intensity of opposition to DuPont was directly proportional to the age of the respondents and inversely
proportional to their level of education. Thus, the
strongest opposition came from people sixty years of
age or older, from illiterate or semiliterate people who
had not finished primary school, and from farmers and
fishermen whose educational level was low and whose
livelihood was directly threatened by the plant. Although all groups in Chang-hua County opposed Du-
Pont, the lowest percentages and least intensity were
found among respondents less than thirty years of age,
those who had completed higher education, students,
teachers, and government workers. Fortunately for Li

---

[46]Interviews with Hsü Han-ch'ing and Wang K'ang-shou.

Fishermen wearing T-shirts with slogan, "I love Lukang, don't want DuPont." An opinion poll taken in July showed that the strongest opposition to DuPont came from older, less educated residents, particularly fishermen. The trio pictured here said they feared a repetition of the "green oyster" affair. (Photo courtesy of *Jen-chien* Magazine)

Tung-liang and his companions, their demonstration seems to have been more popular among intellectuals in Taipei than among the "better" elements closer to home.[47]

The Government's Response

The shock of the June 24 demonstration forced the government in Taipei, which up to this point had studiously

---

[47]*T'ai-ta hsüeh-sheng Tu-pang shih-chien tiao-ch'a-t'uan tsung-ho pao-kao-shu,* 49–51.

Old lady Chi. Although the anti-DuPont organizers were exclusively and Lukang protesters mostly men, a few women like 76-year-old gadfly Mrs. Chi were no less determined to keep the factory out. "If DuPont comes here," she promised, "some of us old folks will protest by drowning ourselves in the sea." (Photo courtesy of *Jen-chien* Magazine)

ignored protests in Lukang, to respond. The DuPont project was unpopular in central Taiwan, and Li's act of civil disobedience gave the story national attention. With the December elections in sight, opposition candidates focused on this issue, while members of the ruling party felt the tide of public opinion running against them. Taipei had to do something to regain the initiative. On July 3, Premier Yu Kuo-hwa announced his decision: Sale of the Chang-pin site to DuPont, which had not yet been sealed, would proceed only after two conditions were met. First, DuPont must submit an "environmental impact assessment" (EIA) (*huan-ching ying-hsiang p'ing-ku*), which would be subject to "strict inspection" by the Environmental Protection Bureau. Second, the relevant government agencies must give a

Premier Yu Kuo-hwa. In July, Premier Yu passed responsibility for resolving the dispute back to the corporation and the community. Temporizing, avoiding conflict, and seeking partial solutions were the hallmark of his regime. (Photo courtesy of the ROC Government Information Office)

full public accounting of plans for the DuPont plant, and the "concerns" of the local residents must be "resolved."[48]

The July 3 decision was typical of Yu Kuo-hwa's approach to government—both its strengths and what many of his critics viewed as its weaknesses. Here as elsewhere, the premier sought to avoid conflict, diffuse tensions, satisfy immediate needs, and delay final resolution of the conflict in hopes that things would work themselves out. In this case, construction was postponed,

---

[48]*Chung-yang jih-pao,* July 4, 1986, 3.

enabling DuPont to go forward in the expectation that a successful environmental impact assessment would lead to approval of the project, and leaving Lukang residents to understand that the plant would not be built until their "concerns" had been "resolved." Yu was buying time for tempers to cool and the search for a permanent solution to proceed.

Cabinet members responsible for policy in this area thought this approach flawed. On July 4, CEPD Chairman Chao Yao-tung told the press that the government must take the initiative to solve such disputes. In Chao's view, Taipei should set standards for acceptable levels of pollution, conduct studies to assess the impact of proposed enterprises, and make authoritative rulings based on the merits of each case—either to prohibit construction, if the safe, clean operation of the factory could not be guaranteed, or to see to it that the factory, once built, performed within the approved guidelines. Chao thought the Ministry of Economic Affairs had mishandled the project and let the conflict with the Lukang residents get out of control. By the time the premier acted, it was already too late. Chao wanted to take charge of this affair, but Yu told him to keep out.

> I (Chao) wanted to discuss the problem with the news reporters, the local people, and government environmental authorities and immediately go with them down to the spot, to use monitors to test whether this factory's air, water, or any kind of pollution was up to international standards. If they were not, I would use my authority to stop the operation. This action would ease the local residents' emotions by showing that the government was not just talking, but really taking action. In this case, only action could solve the problem, not verbal statements. But finally my boss told me, "Mr. Chao,

Chairman of the Council for Economic Planning and Development, Chao Yao-tung. Chao disagreed with Premier Yu's passive approach and wanted to resolve the dispute through more vigorous government action. (Photo courtesy of the ROC Government Information Office)

you'd better keep silent." Therefore, I did not carry out my original approach.[49]

In his own post-mortem, Minister of Economic Affairs Li Ta-hai admitted that he and his ministry had been unprepared for the events in Lukang. But Li believed that even as late as July the government could have

---

[49]Quotation: interview with Chao Yao-tung. Reports of Chao's press conference: *Chung-kuo shih-pao,* July 5, 1986, 3; *Lien-ho pao,* July 5, 1986, 2; *Tzu-li wan-pao,* July 5, 1986, 2; *Chung-kuo shih-pao,* July 6, 1986, 3.

adopted a stronger stand, and he blamed Yu for bowing to the pressure of the mob. Minister Li had differed with the premier on similar cases in the past and found him excessively timid, unwilling to take responsibility or risk confrontation. Li reportedly told Yu that by allowing the Lukang residents an effective veto over this project, "We are only inviting more trouble. No matter what kind of project, definitely some people will be against it. It is always like this." It was better, Li thought, to take a stand, make it stick, and face the consequences.[50]

Although neither cabinet member seemed anxious to defend the premier, both conceded that his options were limited. By the summer of 1986, President Chiang Ching-kuo had signaled his intention to introduce reforms designed to transform Taiwan from an authoritarian to a more democratic form of government. Premier Yu, who might otherwise have followed a more conservative path, could not risk falling out of step with the president or unleashing a chain of events that might lead to repression or violence. Yet the government was ill-equipped to deal with public dissent by legal or administrative means. Taiwan's rapid economic development had produced challenges that could not be met by outmoded governmental institutions, and nowhere was this gap between economy and politics wider than in the areas of environmental protection and public health. "Frankly speaking," Chao Yao-tung later confided,

> the knowledge and experience of our government has not kept up with economic development. The economy moved so fast, but our political movement was far behind. In other words, our economic laws and regulations

---

[50]Interview with Li Ta-hai.

Minister of Economic Affairs, Li Ta-hai. Li's ministry was criticized for approving DuPont's proposal and promising the corporation land in the Chang-pin Industrial Zone. In retrospect, Li defended his ministry's actions and agreed with Chao Yao-tung that the government should have intervened to settle the dispute. (Photo courtesy of the ROC Government Information Office)

did not come out on time. Even now (1988), there are a lot of laws and regulations still in the Legislative Yuan. Suppose you say of the Formosa Plastics plant in Changhua, "It's no good. It's not up to standard." Well, we have no legal standard, no punishments or fines. So how can you take action?[51]

Viewed in this light, Yu Kuo-hwa's move to buy time, during which the bureaucracy could introduce measures

---

[51]Interview with Chao Yao-tung.

to deal with environmental problems and the political institutions could develop channels of communication with local communities, made good sense. For the moment at least, the crisis was defused, while the various parties to the dispute looked for strategies that fit the terms laid down by the premier. For DuPont, this meant winning approval of an environmental impact assessment while improving its public image so that the concerns of the local residents might be resolved. For leaders in Lukang, it meant keeping the movement together and demonstrating on a continuous basis that their concerns were still unmet. And for those agencies of government responsible for industrial development, it meant quietly promoting DuPont's fortunes while avoiding a confrontation with the protesters. The premier's decision had solved nothing, but it provided space in which the parties to the conflict could find their own way out.

Lukang: Keeping the Protest Alive

The success of the June 24 demonstration and the premier's response on July 3 posed new challenges to leaders in Lukang. Just a few days before, Li Tung-liang and the others had labored in obscurity. Now they were in the spotlight. Lukang emerged as a symbol of civic action, at a time when political reforms were being introduced and the standards of public conduct redrawn. Strangers came knocking at Li's door, offering to support the struggle against DuPont, but perhaps also to use it for their own purposes. While civil disobedience had vaulted Lukang to national attention, this tactic was not universally applauded and might not work a second time. Leaders of the Lukang rebellion had won the chance to make a mark on their home-town and on Taiwan as a whole. Now that they had arrived, new choices awaited them.

Beckoning the rebels from one side was the opportunity to make their issue and organization part of a larger movement: to link up with new allies—students, scholars, environmentalists, and opposition politicians—and place the struggle against DuPont on a larger agenda—to clean up and protect Taiwan's natural environment, or, more ambitiously, to use this issue to challenge the monopoly of the Kuomintang regime. The relaxation of political controls begun in the spring of 1986, the formation of the opposition Democratic Progressive Party in September, and the approach of the legislative elections in December made parties and candidates more sensitive to popular issues like environmental protection and more willing to challenge the status quo. Nor did anti-DuPont activists have to go looking for allies. Within days of the demonstration, the nonparty national legislator from Chang-hua County, Hsü Jung-shu, approached Li Tung-liang with an offer to cosponsor a rally that would focus attention on Lukang. As the December elections neared, every candidate in the county, including those on the Kuomintang ticket, came out against the proposed plant. Opposition to the chemical giant was among the most potent political causes in central Taiwan.

Yet the first choice Lukang leaders made—a choice that speaks eloquently for Taiwan's political culture and the atmosphere in which recent reforms are being tested—was to reject participation in the larger political process. Li turned Hsü Jung-shu down flat, refusing even to appear at her rally, which went ahead without local support. The Chang-hua Nuisance Prevention

Association endorsed no candidates in the December elections. At every opportunity, Lukang activists distanced themselves and their movement from the taint of "politics."

This may sound odd, even hypocritical, coming from the likes of Li Tung-liang, who in the past six months had run for and won a seat in the county assembly and mounted one of the largest grass-roots movements in Taiwan's recent history. But leaders of the Lukang rebellion proclaimed a distaste for politics and everything associated with it. In their view, politicians and the political process were so corrupt that any attempt to work with them would engulf and undo otherwise legitimate causes. Candidates would seize an issue to attract a crowd, then harangue their listeners with empty slogans. Elected officials would forget their campaign promises as they moved on to the business of enriching themselves and paying off their supporters. The very term "politics" excluded real commitments to solve real problems. Spokesmen for the anti-DuPont movement felt they had learned this lesson through long experience with the Kuomintang. They considered nonparty and later Democratic Progressive Party members even worse!

When asked about the political leanings of the movement, Li Tung-liang told reporters: "We are not members of any party or faction, or of any particular religion, or of any county or any locale. We just love our hometown and our country and want to protect our environment." Shih Wen-ping struck a similar chord: "We wanted to remain pure and keep environmental protection separate from politics. So whether it is the Kuomintang or the Democratic Progressive Party, we pay no attention to what they are doing. They do their business, and we do ours." Ch'en Ching-hsiang recalls that he agreed to join the protest only after obtaining assurances that it would remain free of politics:

> In the beginning, I told Li Tung-liang, "If you plan to use the anti-DuPont movement for political purposes, then I will announce my withdrawal." At that time, there were many nonparty elements who wanted to join our movement, but we refused, because we had no political intentions. Our only motive was to protect our homeland.[52]

This was the mood that greeted Hsü Jung-shu when she offered to share the platform in Lukang with Li Tung-liang. Li, typically, explained his rejection as an act of high principle: "I wanted to do business, not make trouble. I wanted to do this thing right, to make our country's leaders understand that we were committed to this issue, and not to a political party." Nien Hsi-lin, also typically, was more forthcoming about the jealousy that divided the two groups:

> From the beginning until June 24, Hsü (Jung-shu) had taken no interest whatsoever in the anti-Dupont movement, because she saw no political value in it. Then, suddenly, after the June 24 demonstration, she decided to hold her "explanatory meeting" on June 29. This meant that she was trying to take over leadership of the Lukang movement. And after working on this issue for half a year, we did not want to give up control. Many of the people who were truly committed to Lukang and the movement were suspicious of the nonparty group.[53]

---

[52]Interviews with Li Tung-liang, Shih Wen-ping, and Ch'en Ching-hsiang.

[53]Interview with Li Tung-liang; and first interview with Nien Hsi-lin. For contemporary accounts of discussions between Li Tung-liang and Hsü Jung-shu, see Tzu-li wan-pao, June 27, 1986, 3; and Chung-kuo shih-pao, June 27, 1986, 3. For a description of the June 29 meeting, see Lien-ho pao, July 3, 1986, 3.

Untrusting of politicians and unwilling to enter the larger political arena, leaders in Lukang had to devise other means of keeping their movement alive. The premier had said that construction of the factory could go forward only after the "concerns" of the Lukang residents were "resolved." This gave the rebels power over their own fate, but with that power came the obligation to act. Taipei would be quick to interpret silence as satisfaction and press ahead with the DuPont project. Leaders in Lukang had to find ways to demonstrate on a continuous basis that the people of this city remained firm in their opposition to the Chang-pin plant.

Their solution was to mount periodic events that kept the Lukang public visible and involved. The first of these was a field trip, planned for August 17, to the cadmium-poisoned rice fields of T'ao-yüan County, and, to underline the alternative, a second stop to view the natural beauty of Yangmingshan Park, outside Taipei. Aware of the risks of confrontation, which had already cost the movement some support, Li Tung-liang had agreed to cooperate with local security forces. He had followed advice from the commander of the local draft board (*t'uan-kuan-ch'ü*) to take only four people, rather than the hundreds he had planned, to call on government leaders in Taipei shortly after the June 24 demonstration. He gave local police, military and Kuomintang authorities a full briefing on plans for the August 17 event, two weeks before it was to occur. Li maintains that he accepted all their demands: that the travelers refrain from displaying signs, passing out leaflets, or making speeches, that police officers be assigned to each bus, and that he keep the authorities informed of all his activities. Plans for the trip proceeded smoothly. At 7:00 A.M. on August 17, three hundred Lukang residents waited for chartered buses that were coming from Changhua to take them north. They were wearing T-shirts emblazoned with the slogan "I love Taiwan, don't want Dupont," which had been changed from the original "I love Lukang" to give the movement broader appeal. Everything seemed to be in order.[54]

Then the security forces intervened. Police intercepted the buses on the road from Changhua, preventing them from picking up their charges in Lukang. At the same time, the commander of the Chang-hua army garrison and the Lukang chief of police tried to persuade Li to cancel the trip. Incensed, Li led the crowd on a march toward the county seat. Their advance was blocked by police in full riot gear strung out across the highway. In the confrontation that followed, Li and the security officers squared off, with the would-be travelers and police arrayed behind them. The authorities objected to the T-shirts, whose slogan contained an implicit appeal to people outside Lukang to join what had been a local affair, and insisted the demonstrators change their clothes. "I was born in Lukang and raised in Lukang," Li haughtily replied. "I love my hometown. And yes, I have put on these clothes. If, because I have on these clothes, you cut off my head and my blood flows, I don't care. But I will wear these clothes. 'I love Taiwan.' That's right!" After more than six hours, the two sides

---

[54]Negotiations with draft board commander: *Chung-kuo shih-pao*, June 26, 1986, 3; and June 27, 1986, 3. Although generally translated as "draft board," the *t'uan-kuan-ch'ü* is a regional organization responsible for supervising the civilian-military activities of recruits, reserves, and retired soldiers. It is part of the apparatus that helps maintain domestic security. Events of August 17 were reported in *Lien-ho pao*, August 18, 1986, 3; and *Chung-kuo shih-pao*, August 18, 1986, 3. Other details: interviews with Li Tung-liang and Nien Hsi-lin.

reached an agreement; the Lukang residents would proceed on their journey, wearing their T-shirts, but would visit only T'ao-yüan, after which they would return home, skipping the visit to Taipei. At 1:15 P.M., the buses, loaded with three hundred now wearier protesters, left Lukang.[55]

This confrontation and its outcome demonstrate one of the cardinal features of politics in Taiwan: namely, the "bamboo factor," which enables conflicts to be resolved without violence or an irretrievable loss of face by either side. As with Premier Yu's July 3 decision, there was a good deal of posturing by both parties, followed by a modus vivendi that enabled each of them to get on with his business, while leaving the underlying problem unresolved. Security officials had kept in close contact with Li during the spring and summer of 1986, giving him "friendly" advice to stay out of the DuPont affair while avoiding overt threats or legal sanctions. Colonel Chin Meng-shih, commander of the local draft board, was told to be vigilant, report on the actions and plans of the Lukang protesters, and intervene only in a peaceful way. When Li failed to take their advice, the security units derailed his plans and presented him with an overwhelming force, but one that held an assiduously defensive, even passive posture. Li was angered and insulted by what he considered a double-cross on the part of men who had invited his confidence and by the interruption of legitimate activities by private citizens. The confrontation on August 17 was sharpened by the fact that the security officials were mainlanders and the protesters Taiwanese. Yet with all these tensions, the two sides were willing to stand nose-to-nose for more than six hours under a hot,

---

[55]Quotation: interview with Li Tung-liang.

Police block Lukang protesters. On August 17, police blocked a planned trip by several busloads of Lukang protesters to other parts of Taiwan. (Photo courtesy of *Hsiang-ch'ing* Magazine)

sticky Taiwan sun until they found a way out. When the garrison commander learned that the group's midday meal, paid for and awaiting them on Yangmingshan, would go uneaten, he offered to buy them all lunch.[56]

News of this incident was reported in the national press, which was just what the anti-Dupont forces wanted, since it focused attention on the fact their concerns about pollution remained unresolved. The approach of the December elections served a similar purpose, as nearly all the candidates in Chang-hua County opposed the DuPont plant, and any sign that Taipei might proceed with the project would have hurt the Kuomintang's chances in central Taiwan. Once the elections were

[56]Chin Meng-shih: interview with Steve Chang.

over, however, the situation changed. Observers on all sides expected Taipei to wait until after the elections to give final approval for construction of the plant. This put renewed pressure on the anti-Dupont forces to act.

On December 13, Li Tung-liang organized a trip by more than four hundred Lukang residents, ostensibly to attend a human rights conference in Taipei. Once the caravan of buses was on the road, however, Li unveiled his real objective: to mount a mass demonstration in front of the Presidential Office. The buses, trailed by a carload of security forces, stopped first at the Chiang Kai-shek Memorial to let the travelers stretch their legs and take pictures. Once on the ground, Li led them several blocks to the appointed target, passing out large black placards, which he had prepared beforehand, with the character "complaint" (*yüan*) printed in bold white script. While the protesters stood along the main boulevard holding up their signs, Li and three other representatives went to the Presidential Office to present a copy of their petition, now nine months old and still unanswered, to the officer on duty. After thirty minutes, they returned to the buses and proceeded with their announced itinerary.[57]

This small, brief display was the first mass protest mounted in front of the Presidential Office since the seat of the Republican government had been moved to Taipei in 1949. So shocking was it in the context of Taiwan politics of that time that none of the major

---

[57]The only newspaper report of the December 13 demonstration appeared in *Tzu-li wan-pao*, December 14, 1986, 2. Videotape of the event: "Lukang fan-Tu-pang yün-tung." Other details: interview with Li Tung-liang; and first interview with Nien Hsilin.

Demonstration in front of the Presidential Office. On December 13, Lukang demonstrators led by Li Tung-liang (at left, in suit) displayed signs reading "complaint" [yüan] in the main square in front of the Presidential Office in central Taipei. (Photo courtesy of *Hsiang-ch'ing* Magazine)

Li Tung-liang talks with security agents. While protesters waited, Li asked to deliver their petition to the Presidential Office. (Photo courtesy of *Hsiang-ch'ing* Magazine)

daily newspapers dared report even the bare facts. On this occasion, Li Tung-liang kept his intentions secret from everyone, including his closest advisers. Events of the previous months had taught him that the security forces were determined to undo his plans. He believed that secrecy was essential and that other members of the movement, trusting his leadership, agreed. "No one knew what my plans were," Li later explained. "The people on the bus did not know. They just followed me. Wherever I went they would follow." Li is right that he surprised his fellow travelers, but not everyone liked the idea. "We did not know we were going to the Presidential Office," recalled Ch'en Ching-hsiang, who was on the bus when Li announced his plan. "I said to Li Tung-liang, 'If you are going to the Presidential Office, you should have explained the whole thing ahead of time. You are cheating all of the people on the bus. This is not right.'" Yet Ch'en and the others joined the demonstration, which succeeded in its goal of reminding the government and other observers that the protest in Lukang was still to be reckoned with.[58]

DuPont Makes Its Case

The reaction of DuPont officials to Premier Yu's July 3 statement was mixed. On one hand, they welcomed the opportunity to be judged on the basis of their environmental impact assessment. DuPont had more experience in this area than the ROC government, which had never required a study of this type from anyone and had little idea of what it should contain. The technology to be used in the Chang-pin plant was well established and had caused no problems elsewhere. Insofar as the case was decided on its merits, DuPont expected to win. On the other hand, Yu's promise that the project would not go forward until the "concerns" of the local residents were "resolved" shifted the focus from merits to politics—and this boded ill for DuPont. Company executives believed that this statement demonstrated a failure of leadership. Instead of elevating Taiwan to the standard of modern industrial societies, where important matters are decided by "due process" that allows the public to make its input while reserving for the government the power of final decision, Premier Yu was clinging to the old Chinese system in which "everything is negotiable." In such a system, company sources pointed out, ignorance, prejudice, and emotion could overcome knowledge, analysis, and reason, with unhappy results for Taiwan—and coincidentally for DuPont.

The company's first objective was to develop an environmental impact statement that would demonstrate beyond question that its plant would be clean and safe. This proved more difficult than expected because Taiwan

---

[58]Interviews with Li Tung-liang and Ch'en Ching-hsiang.

had no laws or standards to guide drafters of the document, the form and content of which had to be negotiated in the course of its writing, while the government was pressured to raise or stiffen requirements as they went along. All this left DuPont trying to hit the bull's eye on a moving target. In the end, the company produced a study that, according to one source, was "far more extensive than anything we have to do to build a plant in the United States."

DuPont's other problem was public opinion—how to satisfy the people of Lukang who, under Yu's ground rules, held the black ball. Government officials advised the company to avoid contact with the local community, on the grounds that further publicity would make the problem worse, and argued that many critics of the project were "posturing" for the December elections, after which the resistance would fade. Privately they tried to comfort the Americans with assurances that this was "business as usual in Taiwan." To improve communications, DuPont brought in a veteran employee from the United States, C. K. Chen (Ch'en Ching-kuo), who had grown up in Taiwan, lived for several years in Ch'i-hu, a town just to the south of Lukang, and spoke fluent Taiwanese (min-nan-hua). Chen's mission was to develop a community outreach program that would, as he described it, "convince the local people about the titanium dioxide project." He visited Lukang for the first time in July to meet with leaders of the opposition and moved back to Taiwan permanently in October.[59]

Chen had no greater success with the rebels than Paul Costello had had before him. He found Li Tung-liang and Nien Hsi-lin polite, but inflexible, "opportunists"

---

[59]Interview with C. K. Chen.

who were using the conflict with DuPont for their own political gain and who had in the process been captured by their own forces. "I cannot retreat," Chen quotes Li as telling friends. "I have been carrying the sedan chair, and those who are riding will not let me put my burden down." Nor did the leaders in Lukang think much of DuPont's new spokesman. During their day-long meeting in July, recalled Nien Hsi-lin, "he just tried to convince us. Communication is a two-way exchange, but he treated us like he was the teacher, we were the students, and he was telling us what we should believe."[60]

While private talks hardened feelings on both sides, attempts to present the company's position in public nearly led to violence. Li Tung-liang and Nien Hsi-lin charge that DuPont failed to appear when invited at forums in Lukang, Changhua, and elsewhere, but the evidence shows that company representatives tried to present their case and were shouted down, or worse. Observers at a public meeting sponsored by the Lukang City Council on September 12 describe how a mob gathered outside City Hall and greeted the DuPont delegation with placards condemning the company and with shouts of "Beat them! Beat them!" C. K. Chen claims that his people were told to get out of town and warned that their safety could not be guaranteed if they returned. Even Chang-hua County Magistrate Huang Shih-ch'eng, a close ally of Li Tung-liang who blamed the government for its mismanagement of the Chang-pin project, agreed that DuPont "wanted to talk," but that the protesters "would not listen." "DuPont was trying to communicate,"

---

[60] Interview with C. K. Chen; and second interview with Nien Hsi-lin.

Protesters outside Lukang City Hall. DuPont spokesmen claim that they were denied an opportunity to make their case to the people of Lukang. When they appeared at public meetings, like this one, they were shouted down by protesters inside and outside the hall. (Photo courtesy of *Hsiang-ch'ing* Magazine)

Huang recalled of the Lukang meeting, "but couldn't. The people would not listen. They just didn't want [the plant]."[61]

As these efforts foundered, Chen shifted to a strategy designed to win over the residents of Lukang one by one. He formed a "communications team" of six DuPont employees who were natives of Lukang and had volunteered to go back home to talk to friends, relatives, and other residents about the company, its commitment to its workers and the public, and the proposed plant. After briefings on titanium dioxide and its method of manufacture, the team went to Lukang in September

---

[61]Li and Nien views: interviews with Li Tung-liang and Nien Hsi-lin. Meeting in Lukang: interview with Ch'en Chih-ch'eng. C. K. Chen: interview with C. K. Chen. Huang Shih-ch'eng: interview with Huang Shih-ch'eng.

and began to pass the word that they would like to talk. For the next four months, they met with students, civic organizations, environmental groups, businessmen, fishermen, and anyone else who would see them. "We met in people's homes, in restaurants, hotels, anywhere they were willing to meet us," Chen later explained. "You name it." The approach was direct, personal, and based on testimonies by the DuPont employees about the company, its policies on safety, cleanliness, and civic responsibility. In Chen's view, his team persuaded 80 percent of the people they talked to that the DuPont plant should be built.[62]

Even as the effort in Lukang went forward, however, thinking within the corporation about where to build the titanium dioxide plant was shifting. DuPont Taiwan President Paul Costello was beginning to see that chances for locating the factory in the Chang-pin Industrial Zone were dwindling, and that eventually the plant would have to be built in some other part of Taiwan, if at all. His strategy, as he explained in an interview published in October, was to demonstrate that the proposed project was environmentally sound, so that in the long run it would gain acceptance somewhere on the island.

> If, today, DuPont should leave Lukang, we would take with us the label of "polluter." No matter where we went in Taiwan, we would meet with the same problem. So at present our most important task is to make all the people of Taiwan understand our environmental impact study, to make them understand that DuPont is not a polluter, but on the contrary that we can help Taiwan solve the problem of pollution. If, later, we decide

---

[62]Interview with C. K. Chen.

not to go into Lukang, then we will make that decision on the basis of the situation at that time, and not in response to emotional accusations.[63]

This strategy called for a public relations campaign addressed to a wider audience—one intelligent enough to understand the issues, but far enough removed from the conflict in Lukang to give the company a fair hearing. People of this sort would be impressed if, after review, the government approved DuPont's environmental impact statement. In the meantime, the company tried to reach them with sophisticated newspaper advertisements, a slick, informative brochure, and a series of educational forums in Taipei, Taichung, and other cities outside of Chang-hua County, where spokesmen for DuPont made their case.[64]

The Last Act

By dint of his July 3 statement, Premier Yu had vacated the bench in the DuPont/Lukang dispute and left it to the principals, the corporation and the community, to try their case in the court of public affairs. DuPont could win by proving to the relevant agencies of government and persuading Taiwan's opinion elite that the manufacture of titanium dioxide would be clean and safe. Under the weight of evidence and social consensus, the resistance might break and construction of the plant proceed. The Lukang rebels could win by showing that the local populace remained determined to keep

[63]"Tu-pang tsung-ching-li K'o-ssu-lu," 58.

[64]Newspaper ad: *Chung-kuo shih-pao*, September 15, 1986. The brochure, entitled "Titanium Powder Is Everywhere" ("Wu-so pu-tsai ti t'ai-pai-fen"), was issued on September 22. Other details: Lin Mei-no, "Tu-pang pu-hui ch'ing-yen fang-ch'i," 3.

the factory out of their neighborhood. With the opposition unmoved, DuPont might decide to look for a site elsewhere. After several months, this trial of nerves was resolved by actions that enabled one side to claim victory and the other to deny defeat.

What brought the case to a head were rumors in early 1987 that the company was preparing to submit its environmental impact assessment to the government for approval. The resistance in Lukang had always feared that officials in Taipei would use this legal maneuver as a pretext for authorizing construction of the plant and, with the December elections behind them, simply go ahead. Leaders of the anti-Dupont movement resolved to mount one last event to show that the concerns of the local people were still unanswered.[65]

The event, an "explanation meeting" or rally, was held in Lukang on March 8. The Chang-hua Nuisance Prevention Association, now a recognized legal entity, applied for a permit to hold this meeting in the square facing the T'ien-hou Kung Matsu Temple, the main center of Lukang spiritual and community life. The police rejected this request on the grounds that the gathering would interfere with traffic. After some debate, the two sides reached a compromise: opponents of the plant could hold their rally in a parking lot five hundred meters from the temple, but they should not leave this site or demonstrate outside the parking lot after the meeting ended.

By 9:30 on the morning of March 8, three hundred people gathered to hear Li Tung-liang make a shocking new charge: The manufacture of titanium dioxide was only a cover for the real purpose of the DuPont factory, which was to develop deposits of monazite, an ore containing

---

[65]*Chung-kuo shih-pao*, March 9, 1987, 3.

radioactive materials found along the Taiwan coast, that would be used to make nuclear weapons. The whole thing was a "plot"! When the meeting ended at 11:30, several hundred demonstrators, egged on by Li, broke through the barricades that had been set up around the parking lot and headed down Chung-shan Road, the main street of Lukang, shouting slogans and waving banners and signs attacking DuPont. Using a bullhorn, Lukang Police Chief Hsüeh Chiang-ch'iang warned the crowd to halt its march and disperse, but to no avail. Finally, at the main intersection at Min-ch'üan Road, the demonstrators met a blockade of eighty policemen in full riot gear. The crowd, which vastly outnumbered police, advanced under a head of steam. Young braves in the front began to charge against the line of shields and helmets in an effort to break through. Violence seemed just a slip away.[66]

Then, as quickly as it started, the demonstration was ended by a face-saving compromise of the sort that enables Taiwan politics to bend but not break. Pressed together by determined riot squads on one side and angry demonstrators on the other, Li Tung-liang and the police chief managed to find a simple, workable solution: first the police withdrew from the intersection; then the demonstrators turned, filed down a side street, and looped back to the Matsu Temple, where they dispersed. Within thirty minutes, street life was back to normal.

These events, which made a predictable splash in the Taipei press, forced DuPont's hand. By the spring of 1987, the company's campaign to garner support in Lukang was achieving results, but slowly. C. K. Chen, who headed this effort, saw that his greatest enemy was the clock:

---

[66]The events of March 8 were reported in *Lien-ho pao*, March 9, 1987, 3. In an interview with the author, Ch'en Ching-hsiang confirmed the accuracy of the account of Li's speech.

There was never any doubt in my mind that, given time, we could convince the Lukang people to accept DuPont. The question was, how long did we have? Two years? Three years? Five years? In July 1986, when I made my first trip to Lukang, I sensed that it would be a very tough job to turn the tide within one year. I said to myself, if we have to build this plant within one year, forget it. But given three years, my personal belief at that time was that we had a good chance. We could make it.[67]

If, as Chen reported, the change in Lukang's political climate would take three years, DuPont could not wait. Although they refused to say so in public, by early 1987 company officials had decided to look elsewhere. The opposition in Lukang was too strong and stubborn to be won over quickly. Meanwhile, the government showed no inclination to press ahead with the project. And the Chang-pin Industrial Zone was not the only, or even the best possible, location for the plant. Still, DuPont did not want to withdraw from Chang-hua before its environmental impact assessment was approved, because to do so could be interpreted as an admission that the plant was in fact dangerous and therefore unacceptable anywhere in Taiwan. DuPont's strategy was to hang on, win approval of the EIA, and make a new start in some other part of the island.

One more demonstration in Lukang was not, in itself, lethal—especially since the company did not plan to build there anyway. The problem was that this event put even more pressure on the government, which was already dragging its feet. Drafts of DuPont's environmental impact assessment were shuttled back and forth, as the company made additions and revisions to

---

[67]Interview with C. K. Chen.

meet the government's ballooning demands. "It just kept getting bigger and bigger," one DuPont source recalled. On March 9, the day after the demonstrations in Lukang, a panel of experts convened by the Ministry of Economic Affairs rejected the company's plans for ocean dumping of ferric chloride waste. In the wake of further protests in Lukang, it was hard to see how the government, which had failed to take responsibility for this matter in the past, would risk handing down a favorable decision now. These events effectively reversed the logic underlying DuPont's strategy: Until March, the plan had been to maintain the commitment in Chang-pin until after the EIA was approved, so that the company could not be charged with attempting to build an unsafe plant. With a clean bill of health in hand, DuPont would proceed with construction in Lukang or, if necessary, elsewhere. After March, DuPont executives concluded that the Lukang connection was making it impossible for the government to approve its EIA, no matter how firm the company's guarantees of safety might be. Under these circumstances, the answer was to get out of Lukang, let tempers cool, and hope that the government would then be able to deal with the case on its merits.[68]

On March 12, Paul Costello called a press conference to announce that DuPont would not build its plant in the Chang-pin Industrial Zone, but would submit an environmental impact assessment covering the manufacture of titanium dioxide and seek a new site elsewhere in Taiwan. Costello repeated his conviction that, judged on its merits, the proposed plant would be deemed safe. DuPont had not failed to prove its case, but found it "impossible to communicate on a reasonable basis" with the local populace and thus get a fair hearing for its proposal in any arena. By abandoning

---

[68]MOEA panel of experts: *Chung-kuo shih-pao*, March 10, 1987, 3.

the Chang-pin site, the company hoped "to ensure that examination of the environmental impact assessment is not influenced by popular emotions." DuPont let its option on the property go and accepted the risk that this would be read as an admission of guilt, because it saw that the government could not approve the environmental study until the ruckus in Lukang ended.[69]

Conclusion

On March 22, ten days after DuPont announced its withdrawal, the people of Lukang and supporters from around the island celebrated their victory. That morning, Li Tung-liang burned incense in the T'ien-hou Kung Temple, while Shih Wen-ping read a memorial to the goddess Matsu, reporting their victory and thanking her for support in the struggle against DuPont. The smoke from the burning memorial took this message to the thousand-year-old goddess, another proof of her power to protect the people of the Taiwan Straits. Throughout the day and into the night, thousands of people danced through the streets, calling at shrines, temples, friends, and neighbors to exchange greetings and give thanks. Dragon dancers and marching bands, men on stilts and women in silks, masters of martial arts and religious fetishes, high priests and vagabonds, clowns, magicians, and pyrotechnicians came to mark the defense of old Taiwan against defilement by the forces of modernity. For all those who held Lukang dear, this was the city's finest hour.[70]

Why did the rebellion succeed? There were many circumstantial reasons—the rise of environmental consciousness,

[69]*Lien-ho pao*, March 13, 1987, 3.

[70]*Chung-kuo shih-pao*, March 23, 1987, 3. Colorful footage of the Lukang celebration appears in the video "Lu-kang fan-Tu-pang yün-tung."

the character of the local community, the coincidence of political reforms that made authorities less able or willing to suppress dissent—and perhaps one supernatural factor, the sea-goddess Matsu. But the one element that set Lukang apart from other environmental protests in Taiwan during these years was leadership, in particular that of Li Tung-liang. It was Li who recognized the problem, mobilized the resistance, risked confrontation with the government, and kept up the pressure until DuPont called it quits. No one else in Taiwan had conceived a strategy of this type, pursued it with such single-minded purpose, or achieved such stunning success against such enormous odds. Li brought several weapons to this battle: a record as champion of Lukang causes, a clear vision, a simple message, and a charisma that made his glib statements ring with authenticity. He claimed that people followed him because of the "trust" he had earned through long service to Lukang and, later, because they came to understand the facts about environmental pollution and the threat posed by DuPont. He and other Lukang leaders denied they had ulterior motives. They were simply trying to "save their hometown."

There is another view of Li Tung-liang, one that recognizes his importance in this affair but makes him less a hero. Behind his boyish grin and simple phrases, Li was as much the captive as leader of his troops. Buoyed up by the froth of his own rhetoric, he rode a wave of popular enthusiasm that offered no easy escape. To admit that the proposed factory might, with suitable modifications and guarantees, be made acceptable would have opened Li to accusations that he had been bought off by DuPont or political big-wigs in Taipei, and placed his reputation as champion of Lukang

in jeopardy. To protect himself, he refused to visit Du-
Pont factories in the United States, an experience that
might have softened his views, and intensified his attacks on the company and the government, in the end
charging, with no evidence at all, that the project was
part of a "plot" to manufacture nuclear weapons. After
the June 24 demonstration, if not before, Li had be-
come so deeply and publicly committed to the cause
that he could only go forward, and there was no force in
Lukang or ultimately in Taiwan to stop him.

In retrospect, the rebellion was not unkind to Li
Tung-liang. Following his election as county assemblyman and the growth of his notoriety as Lukang's favor-
ite son, Li's financial standing improved. Formerly the
proprietor of a modest incense shop who drove the family delivery truck, he now heads his own stock company
and owns a big American car—signs, his detractors
say, of some fishy business. On the other hand, Li's
political career seems to have peaked. After the withdrawal by DuPont, Li tried to mount a campaign
against the Taiwan Chemical Factory in Changhua, but
he attracted little support and soon abandoned the effort. His run for the Taiwan Provincial Assembly in
1989 came up short. Li lacks formal education, and
some say he lacks the breadth, the intellect, and perhaps even the ambition to move up the political ladder.
He is, in the end, a Lukang-man, which seems to explain both his success at home and the lack of it in the
world outside.[71]

What drove Li Tung-liang and the others to their moment of triumph? After conceding that both a genuine
concern for the issues and selfish desire for power must
have had something to do with it, was there anything

---

[71]Interview with Ch'en Chih-ch'eng.

else? Some of Li's friends thought so. Nien Hsi-lin, the most clear-sighted and forthcoming of the Lukang insiders, admitted that the attack on DuPont was driven by a desire to settle old scores:

> Let's be frank. In this case, DuPont was the injured party. It is true that we opposed construction of the DuPont plant. But if you want to look deeper, we were using DuPont for other ends. For so long, we had to put up with absurd and intolerable government regulations, while Taiwan had no social movement (that could fight back). Now, in the anti-DuPont movement, we were responding to this whole history of abuse of public authority.[72]

County Magistrate Huang Shih-ch'eng—a Taiwanese, member of the nonparty opposition, mentor and ally of Li Tung-liang, a man with every reason to defend the protesters—found even deeper, darker motives behind the rebellion. For forty-five minutes, in his paneled Changhua office, Huang patiently answered questions about the DuPont affair, criticizing the government and justifying the response from Lukang. Then, without invitation or notice, he launched into a blistering attack on the depravity of (his own) Taiwanese culture and the impossibility of conducting a reasoned public debate (among his own countrymen) on almost any issue. Huang agreed that the opposition to DuPont served as a "pretext" for attacking authorities in Taipei. Sadly, however, he could not say this was a clever strategy or even the product of rational calculation. Rather, it was a mad lashing out at the opposition, a feeding frenzy that seized upon whatever weapons might be at hand. Most people in Taiwan would not consider cleaning up

---

[72]Second interview with Nien Hsi-lin.

**Chang-hua County Magistrate Huang Shih-ch'eng greets Lu-
kang protesters.** Huang, a nonparty [*tang-wai*] Taiwanese with close
ties to Li Tung-liang, publicly supported the protest against DuPont, but
privately questioned the motives of the protesters and the results they
produced. (Photo courtesy of *Hsiang-ch'ing* Magazine)

their own garbage, Huang noted, but they think nothing of attacking others for polluting the environment.
With the relaxation of political controls and the opening
up of debate in Taiwan, the same people had begun to
raise calls for "democracy," even though they were not
democratic themselves and had not the slightest idea
what this term meant, but could use this slogan
against their supposed enemies. There is no way to
satisfy people or solve problems of this type, Huang
concluded, for they are driven by "opposition for its own
sake." "This 'opposition for its own sake' is a basic
problem, very common in Taiwan," Huang explained.
"DuPont is not the only such case. Many problems are
like this. And this makes it difficult to deal with any of
them."[73]

The impact of the Lukang rebellion on developments

---

[73]Quotations: interview with Huang Shih-ch'eng.

in Taiwan as a whole is also subject to more than one interpretation. In a survey of the major events of the 1980s, the Taiwan Social University Cultural and Educational Foundation chose the anti-Dupont movement as one of the ten great enterprises that changed life in Taiwan during that decade.[74] Without doubt, this movement gave a boost to environmental consciousness and organization throughout the island. It established a model for "preventative" action: blocking acts of pollution before they occur, rather than seeking compensation for damages already committed, as had been the case with the "self-salvation" movements of the early 1980s. It showed how local elites can mobilize mass resistance within their communities and reach out to the media and articulate opinion in other parts of the island. It inspired the formation of two organizations— the Green Peace Environmental Workshop (Lü-se Ho-p'ing Kung-tso Shih) and the Taiwan Environmental Protection Alliance (T'ai-wan Huan-ching Pao-hu Lien-meng)—that have given shape and direction to environmental activities in subsequent years. And it publicized the cause of environmental protection in Taiwan and beyond. Leaders of the rebellion have tended, naturally enough, to see great significance in their actions. According to Nien Hsi-lin, the protests

> encouraged the environmental movement throughout Taiwan. We thought, if Lukang fails, it will set the Taiwan environmental movement back ten or twenty years, but if it succeeds, it can give this movement an immediate lift. After Lukang's success, other environmental movements sprang up throughout the island. In addition, Lukang set an example for the labor movement, the farmers' movement, and other social movements in

---

[74]*Lien-ho pao*, December 13, 1990, 15.

Taiwan. As I have said, Lukang was a watershed for politics in Taiwan as a whole.[75]

Yet, listening with another ear, the victory at Lukang has a hollow ring. Spokesmen for DuPont claimed that their investment would bring to central Taiwan greater wealth and opportunity and expose that area to little pollution or other unwanted side effects. The people of Lukang might have tried to find out whether this proposition was true and, if so, whether they could profit by having a titanium dioxide plant in their neighborhood. But blinded by righteous anger, they never gave Du-Pont a chance. Years later, a tour of the city's streets reveals mounds of garbage, streams turned to a thick black soup, and gritty air—all products of public indifference and primitive, highly polluting industries. Li Tung-liang is still chairman of the Chang-hua Nuisance Prevention Association, although, when asked, neither he nor any other member of this organization could cite a current project to clean up their community. Nien Hsi-lin reports that the environmental movement in Chang-hua is dead. In sum, it is not so clear that all the energy spent on resisting DuPont has made Lukang a nicer place to live.[76]

Hsieh Shih-ku, one of the officials who visited DuPont plants in the United States and whose subsequent support for the company did not prevent his rise to the post of speaker of the Chang-hua County Assembly, argues that pollution remains an intractable problem in central Taiwan because of the structure of the local economy and the attitudes of the local inhabitants. Hsieh believes that in the case of large corporations, which are visible, vulnerable, and

---

[75]First interview with Nien Hsi-lin.
[76]Ibid.

have the resources needed to finance their own cleanup, the problem of pollution is being solved. He cites as an example the massive investment made by the Taiwan Chemical Company in Changhua, which, by general consensus, smells much better in 1990 than it did in 1986. A more serious problem lies with the thousands of small household and handicraft factories, particularly those in metal-working and electroplating, that form the backbone of the Chang-hua economy. Every town, every village, and almost every family in the county depends for their livelihood on factories of this type. Their equipment is outmoded, highly polluting, and, if it had to be replaced or fitted for pollution controls, it would be prohibitively expensive. Everyone, or almost everyone, needs these factories, and no one can afford or wants to clean them up.[77]

The problem goes even deeper than this, Hsieh continues, to the attitudes held by owners and neighbors of these small factories and workshops. In his view, Chinese place undue weight on "human feelings" (*jen-ch'ing-wei*), the bonds of interpersonal obligation and concern that govern relations between people and the way they settle their disputes. Because of this penchant, when someone's factory pollutes his neighbor's home, the victim will insist on resolving the problem privately or through an intermediary in a way that preserves relations between the parties, rather than making the matter public. "In my years of experience as an assemblyman," Hsieh confides, "the most serious problem

---

[77]Interview with Hsieh Shih-ku. Hsieh claims that the Taiwan Chemical Company spent NT $2.7 billion (U.S. $100 million) to correct previous problems, which had caused air and water pollution, and that his own factory spent NT $70 million (U.S. $2.6 million) for pollution controls. Even if these figures are exaggerated, they give an idea of the costs, which are beyond the means of most household industries.

in China, which has done the most damage to the nation and to public policy, is the Chinese reliance on *jen-ch'ing-wei.*" "Now in the DuPont case," he adds with a chuckle, "these were foreigners who had no such 'relations' and therefore lacked protection. So the whole thing could explode."[78]

Nor is there convincing evidence that events in Lukang transformed the cause of environmentalism in Taiwan as a whole. Even the country's most ardent environmentalists agree that Taiwan has no "environmental movement"— only environmental episodes. The most noteworthy actions remain periodic outbursts for "self-salvation" that lack articulate leadership, islandwide coordination, and a program for solving past problems or preventing new ones. The communal insularity and refusal to join forces with outside parties and politicians demonstrated in the Lukang case are reflected in the continued fragmentation of environmental politics in Taiwan. Nien Hsi-lin, who left Lukang to work for the Green Peace Environmental Workshop, offering aid and advice to protesters around the island, still considers the defense of the natural environment incompatible with partisan politics. "Those of us who are active in environmental protection have no faith in political parties," notes Nien. "Parties only want votes. They grab onto environmental issues in a short-term, opportunistic way, just to win elections. After the election, they have no interest in the environment." Given such attitudes, which appear to be widespread, it is difficult to see how environmentalism can develop into a coordinated nationwide movement.[79]

Also problematic has been the impact of the Lukang

---

[78]Interview with Hsieh Shih-ku.

[79]Ardent environmentalists: interview with Shih Hsin-min. Nien Hsi-lin quotation: first interview with Nien Hsi-lin.

rebellion on the ROC government and the way Taipei has dealt with environmental protests since 1986. By his own standards, Premier Yu Kuo-hwa had reason to claim that his handling of Lukang was a success. Rather than risk open conflict and the reputation of his government, Yu left the corporation and the community to resolve their dispute, and his strategy worked. Four years later, DuPont was preparing to build its titanium dioxide plant in T'ao-yüan County, while work on the Chang-pin Industrial Zone, slated to receive other tenants, resumed without resistance from local residents. In August 1987, Yu replaced the old EPB with a new Environmental Protection Administration, which received increased funding, personnel, and visibility. During his first eighteen months on the job, EPA Administrator Eugene Chien (Chien Yu-hsin) helped pass twenty-one new laws. The administrative and legal structure needed to design and implement sound environmental policies is taking shape. Meanwhile, annual public and private investment in pollution control in the ROC has more than doubled, from U.S. $900 million in 1986 to $1.9 billion in 1989. Given all this, the premier might feel justified that his "bamboo tactics," bending with the elements, worked, while he and his successor used the time provided to develop a better framework for dealing with such problems in the future.[80]

Yu's critics differed with him at the time, however, and his response to the next major environmental crisis seems to have proven them right. In the summer of 1988, irate farmers and fishermen occupied the Lin-yüan petrochemical complex outside Kaohsiung at the

---

[80]EPA and pollution control investment: *The Economic News*, March 6–12, 1989, 1–3, 7.

southern end of the island. For years, residents of this area had complained that waste from the Lin-yüan refineries was polluting their drinking water, while nothing was being done to solve the problem. Finally, inspired by the example of Lukang and various "self-salvation" movements, villagers seized the complex, barricaded the gates, and demanded compensation. The government, fearing that sabotage would cause massive losses to industries that provide thousands of jobs and billions of dollars in export earnings, forced the companies to make direct cash payments to the demonstrators in exchange for leaving the site and promising not to return. Under this arrangement, eighteen petrochemical companies agreed to pay NT $1.27 billion (U.S. $45.4 million) to individual villagers, with the highest payments reaching NT $80,000 (U.S. $2,850) per person! No money was set aside to correct the problem that provoked the incident, nor did the government take responsibility for policing the cleanup.

Yu Kuo-hwa's detractors saw in Lin-yüan a repetition of the premier's previous errors. Former Minister of Economic Affairs Li Ta-hai found Yu, as usual, too "soft," anxious to avoid confrontation and willing to make compromises. "Lin-yüan is a very bad case," Li complained. "We should spend the money to improve the facilities. But instead we just pass it away to make short-term appeasement, thus inviting people to ask for more, and the money is wasted." Chao Yao-tung, also retired from the cabinet, saw the response at Lin-yüan in the same light: the government had ducked the issue, failed to solve the underlying problems, and worst of all agreed to payoffs that would encourage rebellion in the future. "Lin-yüan is a bomb that could explode anywhere," remarked Chao. "Terrible." Chao charged that the drift in government policy had contributed to a general decline in public morals. He likened the current situation in Taiwan to mainland China under the Red Guards—"Nobody respects the police, nobody believes the government, everybody is against everybody." His explanation, while coming from the opposite end of the political spectrum, was as dark as that offered by Huang Shih-ch'eng:

> Chinese people, if you study Chinese history, are very (hard) to handle. In normal times, they are obedient. They respect senior people, they respect authority. Chinese people are flexible. They can suffer to an extreme that most of the European race cannot imagine. So elastic. But on the other hand, just like a spring, if they get beyond the limit, the Chinese race loses all reason.[81]

Much of the foreign business community also blamed the government for its handling of the Lukang affair. Months passed, and the government refused to render judgment on DuPont's environmental impact assessment, arguing that withdrawal from Lukang made the question moot. DuPont executives saw this as another sign that Taipei had failed to establish rational, workable procedures. "It's fair to say," one source confided, "that industry does not look on the government as having a good handle on the solution to their problems, because they are so political." "We can no longer get things done over here," members of the American Chamber of Commerce complained to the Ministry of Economic Affairs. "If we have a problem, we have to rely on our own wits and our own

---

[81]Quotations: interviews with Li Ta-hai and Chao Yao-tung.

resources. We can no longer rely on the government."[82]

Ironically, DuPont, the apparent loser in Lukang, drew its own lessons from the experience and in some ways may have come out best of all. The company recognized that the level of public concern for the environment, which had long since changed the way DuPont does business in other parts of the world, had now been reached in Taiwan. The lesson, obviously enough, was that the company would have to develop lines of communication to its neighbors in Taiwan and win their understanding and support, just as it has to do elsewhere. "Good is not enough any more," noted C. K. Chen. "You also have to let the people understand. They also have the right to know." Having been caught flat-footed in the Lukang affair, in the future the company would have to act sooner.[83]

This change in attitude has been evident as DuPont seeks to move its titanium dioxide plant to Kuan-yin Township in Tao-yüan County, the site chosen shortly after the decision to withdraw from Chang-hua. Selection of the new location demonstrates the importance the corporation attaches to public opinion. DuPont Taiwan's existing factories, for electronics and pesticides, are both in Tao-yüan, which gives the company an established reputation, source of intelligence, and connections to employees, suppliers, tax collectors, and others who have benefited from association with the American firm. Once the choice was made, DuPont moved immediately to cultivate ties to the

---

[82]Shih Hsin-min, a leading environmental activist, also criticized the government for failing to pass on DuPont's EIA and thus missing the opportunity to establish rational procedures and the rule of law for resolving environmental disputes. Interview with Shih Hsin-min.

[83]Quotation: interview with C. K. Chen.

local community. A twelve-person task force was recruited from among long-time employees of the DuPont factories who were from Kuan-yin or had relatives there and volunteered to speak for the company back home. Team members were divided into native Hakka and Taiwanese speakers and sent to households in Kuan-yin where they had personal or family relations. In these "one-on-one" communications, they emphasized their personal experience with the corporation and invited friends and relatives to visit the DuPont plants. The company hired a public relations firm to contact members of the local assembly, journalists, and county officials and commissioned an independent consultant to draft an environmental impact assessment for the Kuan-yin site. This report, which is *not* required by law (Taiwan now requires an EIA for highly polluting industries, but titanium dioxide is not on the list), projects the impact the factory will have on the environment, as well as its economic benefits in terms of taxes, purchases, and employment. In all these efforts, DuPont has worked quietly and attracted little attention. Attempts to make the project an issue in the December 1989 elections failed. A July 1990 opinion poll shows that two-thirds of the Kuan-yin residents "approve" of the plant or "approve under certain conditions." By the end of 1990, DuPont had received a "site preparation permit" and began grading, laying drainage pipe, and putting up fences. The company expected to begin construction soon.[84]

---

[84]For an account of DuPont's program in Kuan-yin, see "DuPont Soothes Tempers by Involving Taiwanese," *Business Asia* (July 1990). Public relations firm: interview with Steve Chang. EIA: "T'ai-wan Tu-pang ku-fen yu-hsien kung-szu erh-yang-hua-t'ai-ch'ang chien-ch'ang huan-ching ying-hsiang p'ing-ku pao-kao." Public opinion poll: "Kuan-yin-hsiang hsiang-min tui Tu-pang kung-szu tsai Kuan-yin-hsiang she-ch'ang chih i-chien."

POSTSCRIPT

IN THE SPRING of 1991, as I was preparing this manuscript for publication, the publisher of this series, Douglas Merwin, brought to my attention an article in the *New York Times*[1] that reassured me that the story of Lukang, while somewhat distant from many of my prospective readers, has resonances nearer to home.

The *Times* report described the battle raging in Wallace, Louisiana, a fallen plantation town on the banks of the Mississippi, thirty miles upstream from New Orleans. The people of Wallace, or at least some of them, have grown alarmed by news that Formosa Plastics (the largest private corporation in Taiwan and the parent body of the Taiwan Chemical Factory in Changhua) plans to build a $700 million factory for processing wood pulp and manufacturing rayon amid the tranquil landscape and historic houses of this backwater bayou community. River Road, which meanders through Wallace and surrounding Saint John the Baptist Parish, is known to tourists for its antebellum plantation homes and to medical researchers and the general public as "Cancer Alley." In the past, Wallace escaped the industrialization that most people believe has caused the high cancer rates in this part of Louisiana. Now,

---

[1] *New York Times*, April 9, 1991, A16.

environmentalists, historic preservationists, and citizen groups in Wallace have joined the bitter fight to keep Formosa Plastics out.

Formosa Plastics has been supported by Louisiana Governor Buddy Roemer and by local business and political interests, mostly white, who stand to profit from the new investment. The Taiwan company has purchased 1,740 acres in the Wallace area, including an old rice and sugar planation. This land, once reserved for agricultural and residential use, was rezoned for industry in a stormy meeting of the Parish Council. The plant's defenders argue that Wallace needs the seven hundred jobs Formosa Plastics promises to provide. In the past, industry was welcomed to this region, no questions asked; jobs and tax dollars were all the locals wanted. Even critics of the new plant agree the area still needs jobs, but economic motives have been eclipsed by concerns over health, the environment, and the character of the Wallace community.

Wilfred M. Greene, a black retired school principal who has been approached by Formosa Plastics to sell the riverfront land that his ancestors, plantation workers, bought in 1874, turned the company down. Mr. Greene, sixty-eight, who claims he only wants to live out his years in peace, notes that in the struggle over the plant something basic in the community has changed. "Whatever happens, it will never be business as usual in St. John Parish again," he told a reporter. "Politicians here never once dreamed this plant would drum up this much opposition. They will never try this again."

APPENDIX 1
United Daily News Telephone Poll of Taipei Residents, July 1986

During the first week of July 1986, shortly after the June 24 demonstration in Lukang, the *United Daily News* conducted a telephone poll of 318 residents of the Taipei area, selected at random from the telephone book. Each respondent was asked ten questions about environmental protection, government policy, and the events in Lukang. The results were published in *United Daily News* on July 7.

1. Recently, Premier Yu Kuo-hwa said that the goal of future policy will be to "give equal emphasis to economic development and environmental protection." Do you believe this statement?

Believe	55.0%
Do not believe	15.7%
Don't know/no opinion	29.2%

2. In your opinion, is the government doing a good or bad job in the area of pollution control?

Good	20.1%
Bad	61.6%
Uncertain	9.1%
Don't know/no opinion	9.1%

3. In your opinion, which is more important, economic development or environmental protection?

Economic development	7.9%
Environmental protection	30.8%
Uncertain	2.5%
Don't know/no opinion	3.8%
Both are important	55.0%

4. In your opinion, is there a conflict between these two [goals]?

Yes	28.6%
No	50.0%
Uncertain	10.1%
Don't know/no opinion	11.3%

5. Some people say that at the present time the government places priority on developing the economy. Others say that the government places more emphasis on environmental protection. Which do you think the government emphasizes?

Developing the economy	52.8%
Protecting the environment	12.6%
Uncertain	4.7%
Don't know/no opinion	1.5%
Equal emphasis on both	15.4%

6. Do you agree with the saying of the Lukang people, "We love Lukang, don't want DuPont"?

Agree	34.3%
Disagree	25.2%
Uncertain	10.1%
No opinion	15.4%
Have not heard of that	15.1%

7. Do you approve of the Lukang people's protest petition and their methods of opposing construction of the DuPont plant?

Approve	40.3%
Disapprove	28.0%
Uncertain	8.5%
No opinion	11.0%
Have not heard of the affair	12.3%

8. In your opinion, has communication between government officials and the Lukang people on the construction of the DuPont plant been handled well?

Yes	11.9%
No	35.5%
Don't know/no opinion	52.5%

9. The government has said that if DuPont builds a plant in Lukang, it will require that DuPont apply strict pollution controls. In your opinion, can the government perform this task?

Yes	37.1%
No	22.3%
Uncertain	23.0%
Don't know/no opinion	17.6%

10. If DuPont can provide guarantees that it will completely eliminate pollution, would you approve of DuPont building a plant in Lukang?

Yes	49.8%
No	20.2%
Uncertain	11.4%
No opinion	18.6%

APPENDIX 2
National Taiwan University Student Poll of Chang-hua County Residents, July 1986

From July 1 to July 18, 1986, the National Taiwan University Students DuPont Affair Investigation Team collected data on public opinion in Chang-hua County, regarding the plan to locate a DuPont chemical plant in the Chang-pin Industrial Zone and the movement to block construction of that plant. The 447 respondents to this poll were selected by the following method: Student pollsters started at the main intersection in the center of Lukang (Chung-shan Road and Min-tsu Road) and spread outward on both sides of the street, taking an interview at every 10 houses, altogether 147 subjects. In Changhua City, they chose the county government building, the train station, the Yang-ming Middle School, and the Taiwan Chemical Factory as the four starting points, proceeding outward along both sides of the street, stopping at every 10 houses, altogether 58 subjects. In several smaller towns and villages, they took random samples of residents, altogether 242 subjects. The results of this poll appeared in *T'ai-ta hsüeh-sheng Tu-pang shih-chien tiao-ch'a-t'uan tsung-ho pao-kao-shu.*

I. Basic Demographic Data

1. Sex

Male	309 persons	69%
Female	138	31%
Total	447	100%

2. Age

14–20	47 persons	11%
21–30	99	22%
31–40	117	26%
41–50	73	16%
51–60	59	13%
61–up	51	11%
Total	446	100%

3. Profession

Government	7 persons	2%
Education	7	2%
Labor	63	14%
Military	0	0%
Commerce	144	32%
Farmer	65	15%
Fishing	57	13%
Student	38	9%
Retired	16	4%
Independent	9	2%
Housewife	34	8%
Undetermined	3	1%
Total	443	100%

4. Education

None	57 persons	13%
Literate	21	5%
Elementary	156	35%
Lower Middle	78	17%
Upper Middle	103	23%
Higher	31	7%
Total	446	100%

5. Region

Lukang City	147 persons	33%
Lukang suburbs	52	12%
Fu-hsing Township	54	12%
Hsien-hsi Township	30	7%
Shen-kang Township	54	12%
Fang-yüan Township	52	12%
Changhua City	58	13%
Total	447	100%

II. Responses to Questions

1. Do you know that the DuPont Corporation intends to set up a titanium dioxide factory in the Chang-pin Industrial Zone?

Know	93%
Do not know	7%

2. When you found out that the DuPont Corporation wanted to set up a factory, what was your reaction?

Strongly approved	0 persons	0%
Approved	15	4%
Opposed	117	28%
Strongly opposed	255	62%
No opinion	26	6%
Missing cases	(34)	—
Total	413	100%

The 15 respondents who approved of the DuPont plant gave the following reasons for taking this position (note that each respondent could give more than one reason):

73%	"Help Taiwan's economic development, raise the level of industry."
	"DuPont can do good antipollution work and set an example for others."
40%	"Increase local employment, enrich local economy."
27%	"Improve local public works (roads, etc.)."
13%	"Increase my own income."

The 372 respondents who opposed the DuPont plant gave the following reasons (note that each respondent could give more than one reason):

94%	"The DuPont plant can pollute the natural environment."
88%	"The DuPont plant can cause chronic poisoning of human beings."
69%	"Fear of accident similar to Bhopal."

60%	"The plant could harm the standard of living and lower personal income."
55%	"The plant could harm local cultural objects and the tourist industry."
4%	"DuPont is an American company."

3. What is your view of the demonstration that took place on Lukang's Chung-shan Road on June 24?

Strongly approve	117 people	29%
Approve	111	27%
Strongly disapprove	3	1%
Disapprove	26	6%
No opinion	123	30%
Don't know	27	7%
Missing cases	(40)	—
Total	407	100%

4. Do you believe that if DuPont sets up a factory here, it will definitely create pollution?

Yes, definitely	309 people	75%
Not necessarily, if proper precautions are taken, pollution can be prevented	62	15%
No, it will not cause pollution	3	1%
Don't know	34	8%
Other	4	1%
Missing cases	(35)	—
Total	412	100%

5. If the Ministry of Economic Affairs were to publish a research report on the titanium dioxide factory, would you believe it?

Strongly believe	6 people	1%
Believe	44	11%
Doubt	168	41%
Strongly doubt	135	33%
No opinion	58	14%
Don't know	1	0%
Missing cases	(35)	—
Total	412	100%

6. In your opinion, what would be the best way to resolve the DuPont factory case?

Let the central government decide	17 people	4%
Let the Chang-hua County government or Assembly and the central government decide	48	12%
Hold local referendum	243	61%
Hold national referendum	53	13%
No opinion	25	6%
Other	11	3%
Missing cases	(50)	—
Total	397	100%

7. If, in the end, the DuPont Corporation decides to build a plant in the Chang-pin Industrial Zone, what measures would you take?

Oppose it to the death	65 people	16%
Damage the DuPont factory's construction work	19	5%
Show dissatisfaction by public demonstration	35	9%
Demand and oversee effective pollution prevention work by DuPont	113	28%
Express welcome	4	1%
Move residence	60	15%
Take no action	74	19%
Other	27	7%
Missing cases	(50)	—
Total	397	100%

8. Do you approve of polluting the living (human) environment in order to earn money?

Strongly approve	3 people	1%
Approve	1	0%
Oppose	98	24%
Strongly oppose	300	73%
No opinion	10	2%
Don't know	1	0%
Missing cases	(34)	—
Total	413	100%

9. What is your basic estimate of the anti-DuPont activities in this place, up to the present time?

People have done a good job of protecting their own environment	136 people	33%
People still have not done enough to protect their own environment	169	42%
A few politicians are trying to promote their own political interests	10	2%
Opportunists are taking advantage of the situation to provoke public opinion and divide feelings between the government and people	3	1%
These are the emotional and irrational actions of the people	19	4%
No opinion	51	13%
Don't know	12	3%
Other	7	2%
Missing cases	(40)	—
Total	407	100%

III. Strength of Opposition by Demographic Factors

1. Age

Age group	Number of people	Opposed	Strongly opposed	Total opposed
14–20	44	25.0%	52.3%	77.3%
21–30	95	41.1%	48.4%	89.5%
31–40	112	24.1%	67.0%	91.1%
41–50	70	22.9%	70.0%	92.9%
51–60	52	26.9%	63.5%	90.4%
61–up	40	25.0%	70.0%	95.0%
Total	413	28.3%	61.4%	89.7%

2. Education

Level of education	Number of people	Opposed	Strongly opposed	Total opposed
Illiterate	45	28.9%	66.7%	95.6%
Literate	19	10.5%	89.5%	100.0%
Elementary	142	21.8%	71.1%	92.9%
Lower middle	74	36.5%	53.8%	90.3%
Upper middle	102	29.4%	52.4%	81.8%
Higher	30	46.7%	29.0%	75.7%
Total	412	28.3%	61.4%	89.7%

3. Region

Region	Number of people	Opposed	Strongly opposed	Total opposed
Lukang City	145	26.2%	66.2%	92.4%
Lukang suburbs	52	25.0%	71.2%	96.2%

Fu-hsing Township	50	20.0%	80.0%	100.0%
Hsien-hsi Township.	25	40.0%	40.0%	80.0%
Shen-kang Township	47	27.7%	51.1%	78.8%
Fang-yüan Township	44	25.0%	63.6%	88.6%
Changhua City	51	43.1%	41.2%	84.3%
Total	414	28.3%	61.8%	90.1%

4. Profession

Profession	Number of people	Opposed	Strongly opposed	Total opposed
Fishermen	51	7.8%	86.3%	94.1%
Workers	58	25.9%	63.8%	89.7%
Housewives	31	29.0%	67.8%	96.8%
Retired	13	38.5%	61.5%	100.0%
Merchants	138	31.9%	58.7%	90.6%
Farmers	60	31.7%	58.3%	90.0%
Independent	9	22.2%	55.6%	77.8%
Students	36	30.6%	52.8%	83.4%
Education	5	40.0%	40.0%	80.0%
Government	7	57.1%	14.3%	71.4%
Undetermined	3	33.3%	33.3%	66.6%
Total	411	28.2%	61.8%	90.0%

GLOSSARY

Chang-hua 彰化

Chang-hua hsien kung-hai fang-chih hsieh-hui 彰化縣公害防治協會

Chang-hua pin-hai kung-yeh ch'ü 彰化濱海工業區

Chao Yao-tung 趙耀東

chen [township] 鎮

Ch'en Chih-ch'eng 陳志成

ch'en-ch'ing 陳請

Ch'en Ching-hsiang 陳景祥

Ch'en Ch'ing-kuo 陳慶國

Ch'i-hu 溪湖

Chien Yu-hsin 簡又新

Chin Meng-shih 金夢石

ching-ch'eng so-chih, chin-shih
 wei-k'ai　　精誠所至金石為開

Chuang Chin-yüan　　莊進源

Chung-kuo shih-pao　　中國時報

Chung-shan Road　　中山路

Chung-yang jih-pao　　中央日報

Hsiang-ch'ing yüeh-k'an　　鄉情月刊

Hsiao Hsin-huang　　蕭新煌

Hsieh Shih-ku　　謝式穀

Hsin-chu　　新竹

Hsü Chih-k'un　　許志錕

Hsü Han-ch'ing　　許漢卿

Hsü Jung-shu　　許榮淑

Hsü Kuo-an　　徐國安

Hsüeh Chiang-ch'iang　　薛江墻

Hua-t'an　　花壇

huan-ching ying-hsiang p'ing-ku　環境影響評估

Huang Chin-mu　　黃金木

Huang Shih-ch'eng	黃石城
Hwang Tzuen-chiou	黃尊秋
Jen-chien	人間
jen-ch'ing-wei	人情味
jen-yen k'o-wei	人言可畏
Jung-min kung-ch'eng-ch'u	榮民工程處
Ku Chen-fu	韋振甫
Kuan-yin	觀音鄉
Li Ta-hai	李達海
Li Tung-liang	李棟樑
Lien-ho pao	聯合報
Lin-yüan	林園
Liu Tu-hsing	劉篤行
Lü-se ho-p'ing kung-tso shih	綠色和平工作室
Lukang	鹿港
Matsu	媽祖
Meng-chia	艋舺

Min-ch'üan Road 民權路

min-nan-hua 閩南話

Nien Hsi-lin 粘錫麟

Shih Ch'i-yang 施啓揚

Shih Hsin-min 施信民

Shih Wen-ping 施文炳

T'ai-wan huan-ching
pao-hu lien-meng 台灣環境保護聯盟

tang-wai 黨外

T'ao-yüan 桃園

T'ien-hou Kung 天后宮

T'ien-hsia 天下

Tsou Ch'ao-hua 鄒超華

t'uan-kuan-ch'ü 團管區

T'ui-ch'u i-kuan-ping
fu-tao wei-yüan-hui 退除役官兵輔導委員會

t'ung [related] 同

tzu-li chiu-chi 自力救濟

Tzu-li wan-pao	自立晚報
Tzu-yu jih-pao	自由日報
Wang Chih-kang	王志剛
Wang Fu-ju	王福入
Wang K'ang-shou	王康壽
Wen-wu Temple	文武廟
Wu Ta-yu	吳大猷
Yeh Wan-ch'ung	葉萬崇
Yu Kuo-hwa	俞國華
yüan [complaint]	怨

BIBLIOGRAPHY

Newspapers

Chung-kuo shih-pao (China times)
Chung-yang jih-pao (Central daily news)
Lien-ho pao (United daily news)
Tzu-li wan-pao (Independent evening press)
Tzu-yu jih-pao (Freedom daily)

Periodicals

Economic News
Hsiang-ch'ing yüeh-k'an (Hometown affairs monthly). Lukang: Chang-hua County Nuisance Prevention Association, 1986–87.
Jen-chien (Among the people)
T'ien-hsia (Commonwealth)

Books and Articles

Ch'i-shih nien-tai fan-wu-jan tzu-li chiu-chi ti chieh-kou yü kuo-ch'eng fen-hsi (Analysis of the structure and process of anti-pollution self-salvation in the 1970s). Edited by Hsiao Hsin-huang. Taipei: Huan-ching pao-hu she, 1988.
Chung-hua min-kuo ch'i-shih-ch'i-nien Chang-hua-hsien t'ung-chi yao-lan (Statistical overview of Chang-hua County for 1988). Edited by the Chang-hua County Government. Changhua, June 1988.

Deglopper, Donald. "Artisan Work and Life in Taiwan." *Modern China* 5, 3 (July 1979), 283–316.

------. "Doing Business in Lukang." In *Economic Organization in Chinese Society*, edited by W. E.Willmott. Stanford: Stanford University Press, 1972.

------. "Lu-kang: A City and Its Trading System." In *China's Island Frontier: Studies in Historical Geography of Taiwan*, edited by Ronald G. Knapp. Honolulu: University of Hawaii Press, 1980.

------. "Religion and Ritual in Lukang." In *Religion and Ritual in Chinese Society*, edited by Arthur P. Wolf. Stanford: Stanford University Press, 1974.

------. "Social Structure in a Nineteenth-Century Taiwanese Port City." In *The City in Late Imperial China*, edited by William G. Skinner. Stanford: Stanford University Press, 1977.

Hsiao Hsin-huang. *Wo-men chih yu i-ke T'ai-wan* (We only have one Taiwan). Taipei: Yüan-shan ch'u-pan-she, 1987.

T'ai-Min ti-ch'ü jen-k'ou t'ung-chi, 1987 (1987 Taiwan-Fukien demographic fact book). Taipei: ROC Ministry of the Interior, December 1988.

T'ai-ta hsüeh-sheng Tu-pang shih-chien tiao-ch'a-t'uan tsung-ho pao-kao-shu (Summary report of the National Taiwan University students DuPont affair investigation team). Taipei: Niu-tun ch'u-pan-she, 1986.

Won, Tai-sheng. "Environmental Awareness Stimulates Grass Roots Democracy: Environmental Protest and a New Citizen Movement in Taiwan—A Case-study of the Anti-DuPont Movement." M.S. thesis, State University of New York at Buffalo, May 31, 1987.

Videotape

"Lu-kang fan-Tu-pang yün-tung" (The Lukang anti-DuPont movement). No. 8 in series, "Tai-wan chiu-shih che-yang chang-ta ti" (That is how Taiwan has grown up). Taipei: Min-chin chou-k'an.

Unpublished Reports

Chuang Chin-yüan et al. "K'ao-ch'a Mei-kuo Tu-pang kung-szu

erh-yang-hua-t'ai kung-ch'ang wu-jan k'ung-chih she-shih
pao-kao-shu" (Report on an investigation into the American
DuPont Corporation's titanium dioxide factory pollution control facilities). Taipei: Environmental Protection Bureau, 1986.
T'ai-hsing kung-ch'eng ku-wen ku-fen yu-hsien kung-szu (T'ai-
hsing Engineering Consultant Company, Ltd.). "T'ai-wan Tu-
pang ku-fen yu-hsien kung-szu erh-yang-hua-t'ai-ch'ang
chien-ch'ang huan-ching ying-hsiang p'ing-ku pao-kao (chai-
yao-pen)" (Environmental impact assessment report for construction of the DuPont Taiwan Ltd. titanium dioxide factory
[abstract]). July 1988.
T'ao-yüan huan-ching pao-hu chi-chin-hui (T'ao-yüan Environmental Protection Foundation). "Kuan-yin-hsiang hsiang-min
tui Tu-pang kung-szu tsai Kuan-yin-hsiang she-ch'ang chih
i-chien" (Attitudes of the residents of Kuan-yin Township toward establishment of the DuPont factory in Kuan-yin Township).

Interviews

Note: Identification following interviewee's name is the
office or position he held at the time of the Lukang
affair, 1985–87.

Chang, Steve (Chang Ya-ch'ing). President, Steve Chang and As-
sociates. Taipei, December 13, 1990.
Chao Yao-tung. Chairman, Council for Economic Planning and
Development. Taipei, November 18, 1988.
Ch'en Chih-ch'eng. Lukang correspondent, *Chung-kuo shih-pao*.
Changhua, December 14, 1990.
Ch'en Ching-hsiang. Director, Chang-hua County Fishermen's
Association. Lukang, December 23, 1988.
Chen, C. K. (Ch'en Ching-kuo). Unit Manager for Business Ser-
vices, DuPont Taiwan, Ltd. Taipei, December 14, 1990.
Chuang Chin-yüan. Director, Environmental Protection Bureau.
Taipei, November 21, 1988.
Hsieh Shih-ku. Deputy Speaker, Chang-hua County Assembly.
Changhua, December 14, 1990.
Hsü Chih-k'un. National Assemblyman. Lukang, December 14,
1990.
Hsü Han-ch'ing. Teacher, Lukang Middle School. Lukang, De-
cember 23, 1988.

Hsü Kuo-an. Director, Industrial Development Bureau, Ministry of Economic Affairs. Taipei, November 15, 1988.

Huang Chin-mu. Chairman, Lukang Rotary Club. Lukang, December 23, 1988.

Huang Shih-ch'eng. Magistrate, Chang-hua County. Changhua, November 16, 1988.

Li Ta-hai. Minister of Economic Affairs. Taipei, November 14, 1988.

Li Tung-liang. Chairman, Chang-hua County Nuisance Prevention Association. Changhua, November 16, 1988.

Liu, David (Liu Tu-hsing). Manager for Corporate Communications, DuPont Taiwan Ltd. Taipei, October 26, 1988.

Nien Hsi-lin. Secretary, Chang-hua County Nuisance Prevention Association. Taipei, November 4 and 17, 1990.

Shih Hsin-min. Chairman, Taiwan Environmental Protection Alliance. Taipei, October 27, 1988.

Shih Wen-ping. Chairman, Wen-k'ai Poetry Society. Lukang, December 23, 1988.

Wang Fu-ju. Mayor of Lukang. Lukang, December 14, 1990

Wang K'ang-shou. Teacher, Lukang Middle School. Lukang, December 14, 1990.

Yeh Wan-ch'ung. Speaker, Lukang City Council. Changhua, December 14, 1990.

INDEX

Bhopal, India, 12, 22, 102

Chang-hua County
Fishermen's Association,
13, 19, 31
Chang-hua County Nuisance
Prevention Association,
31, 59, 75, 85
Chang-pin Industrial Zone
(CPIZ), vii; selected by
DuPont, 7; photo of, 8;
and local fishermen,
19–20, 29; first news of
planned construction in,
25; DuPont plans for,
33–34, 73, 77–78; recent
activities in, 88; polling
about, 99, 101, 105
Chao Yao-tung, 10, 54–56;
89–90
Chen, C.K. (Ch'en Ching-kuo),
70–73
Ch'en Chih-ch'eng, 37–38
Ch'en Ching-hsiang, 13, 31,
61, 68
ch'en-ch'ing (petition), 27
Chiang Ching-kuo, President,
8, 56
Chien, Eugene (Chien
Yu-hsin), 88
Chin Meng-shih, 64
China Times (*Chung-kuo
shih-pao*), 37, 46
Chuang Chin-yüan, 6, 37
conservation movement, 11

Costello, Paul, 33–35; photo
of, 34; 70, 73, 78
Council for Economic
Planning and
Development (CEPD), 10,
54

Democratic Progressive Party
(DPP), 59–60
draft board (*t'uan-kuan-ch'ü*)
62–64
"environmental impact
assessment" (EIA), 6;
required of DuPont, 52,
54, 58; DuPont seeks to
produce, 69, 73–79; for
T'ao-yüan site, 90–92
Environmental Protection
Administration, 88
Environmental Protection
Bureau (EPB), 6, 37, 52,
88
Executive Yuan, 33

Formosa Plastics Corporation,
6, 10, 57, 93–94

Gardner, Matthew M., ix
"green oyster" affair, 12,
20–21, 51
Green Peace Environmental
Workshop, 84, 87
Greene, Wilfred M., 94

Hsieh Shih-ku, 37, 85–86

119

STUDIES OF THE EAST ASIAN INSTITUTE

The Ladder of Success in Imperial China, by Ping-ti Ho. New York: Columbia University Press, 1962.

The Chinese Inflation, 1937-1949, by Shun-hsin Chou. New York: Columbia University Press, 1963.

Reformer in Modern China: Chang Chien, 1853-1926, by Samuel Chu. New York: Columbia University Press, 1965.

Research in Japanese Sources: A Guide, by Herschel Webb with the assistance of Marleigh Ryan. New York: Columbia University Press, 1965.

Society and Education in Japan, by Herbert Passin. New York: Teachers College Press, 1965.

Agricultural Production and Economic Development in Japan, 1873-1922, by James I. Nakamura. Princeton: Princeton University Press, 1967.

Japan's First Modern Novel: Ukigumo of Futabatei Shimel, by Marleigh Ryan. New York: Columbia University Press, 1967.

The Korean Communist Movement, 1918-1948, by Dae-Sook Suh. Princeton: Princeton University Press, 1967.

The First Vietnam Crisis, by Melvin Gurtov. New York: Columbia University Press, 1967.

Cadres, Bureaucracy, and Political Power in Communist China, by A. Doak Barnett. New York: Columbia University Press, 1968.

The Japanese Imperial Institution in the Tokugawa Period, by Herschel Webb. New York: Columbia University Press, 1968.

Higher Education and Business Recruitment in Japan, by Koya Azumi. New York: Teachers College Press, 1969.

The Communists and Peasant Rebellions: A Study in the Rewriting of Chinese History, by James P. Harrison, Jr. New York: Atheneum, 1969.

How the Conservatives Rule Japan, by Nathaniel B. Thayer. Princeton: Princeton University Press, 1969.

Aspects of Chinese Education, edited by C.T. Hu. New York: Teachers College Press, 1970.

Documents of Korean Communism, 1918-1948, by Dae-Sook Suh. Princeton: Princeton University Press, 1970.

Japanese Education: A Bibliography of Materials in the English Language, by Herbert Passin. New York: Teachers College Press, 1970.

Economic Development and the Labor Market in Japan, by Koji Taira. New York: Columbia University Press, 1970.

The Japanese Oligarchy and the Russo-Japanese War, by Shumpei Okamoto. New York: Columbia University Press, 1970.

Imperial Restoration in Medieval Japan, by H. Paul Varley. New York: Columbia University Press, 1971.

Japan's Postwar Defense Policy, 1947-1968, by Martin E. Weinstein. New York: Columbia University Press, 1971.

Election Campaigning Japanese Style, by Gerald L. Curtis. New York: Columbia University Press, 1971.

China and Russia: The "Great Game," by O. Edmund Clubb. New York: Columbia University Press, 1971.

Money and Monetary Policy in Communist China, by Katharine Huang Hsiao. New York: Columbia University Press, 1971.

The District Magistrate in Late Imperial China, by John R. Watt. New York: Columbia University Press, 1972.

Law and Policy in China's Foreign Relations: A Study of Attitude and Practice, by James C. Hsiung. New York: Columbia University Press, 1972.

Pearl Harbor as History: Japanese-American Relations, 1931-1941, edited by Dorothy Borg and Shumpei Okamoto, with the assistance of Dale K. A. Finlayson. New York: Columbia University Press, 1973.

Japanese Culture: A Short History, by H. Paul Varley. New York: Praeger, 1973.

Doctors in Politics: The Political Life of the Japan Medical Association, by William E. Steslicke. New York: Praeger, 1973.

The Japan Teachers Union: A Radical Interest Group in Japanese Politics, by Donald Ray Thurston. Princeton: Princeton University Press, 1973.

Japan's Foreign Policy, 1868-1941: A Research Guide, edited by James William Morley. New York: Columbia University Press, 1974.

Palace and Politics in Prewar Japan, by David Anson Titus. New York: Columbia University Press, 1974.

The Idea of China: Essays in Geographic Myth and Theory, by Andrew March. Devon, England: David and Charles, 1974.

Origins of the Cultural Revolution: I, Contradictions Among the People, 1956-1957, by Roderick MacFarquhar. New York: Columbia University Press, 1974.

Shiba Khan: Artist, Innovator, and Pioneer in the Westernization of Japan, by Calvin L. French. Tokyo: Weatherhill, 1974.

Insei: Abdicated Sovereigns in the Politics of Late Heian Japan, by G. Cameron Hurst. New York: Columbia University Press, 1975.

Embassy at War, by Harold Joyce Noble. Edited with an introduction by Frank Baldwin, Jr. Seattle: University of Washington Press, 1975.

Rebels and Bureaucrats: China's December 9ers, by John Israel and Donald W. Klein. Berkeley: University of California Press, 1975.

Deterrent Diplomacy, edited by James William Morley. New York: Columbia University Press, 1976.

House United, House Divided: The Chinese Family in Taiwan, by Myron L. Cohen. New York: Columbia University Press, 1976.

Escape from Predicament: Neo-Confucianism and China's Evolving Political Culture, by Thomas A. Metzger. New York: Columbia University Press, 1976.

Cadres, Commanders, and Commissars: The Training of the Chinese Communist Leadership, 1920-45, by Jane L. Price. Boulder, CO: Westview Press, 1976.

Sun Yat-sen: Frustrated Patriot, by C. Martin Wilbur. New York: Columbia University Press, 1977.

Japanese International Negotiating Style, by Michael Blaker. New

York: Columbia University Press, 1977.

Contemporary Japanese Budget Politics, by John Creighton Campbell. Berkeley: University of California Press, 1977.

The Medieval Chinese Oligarchy, by David Johnson. Boulder, CO: Westview Press, 1977.

The Arms of Kiangnan: Modernization in the Chinese Ordnance Industry, 1860–1895, by Thomas L. Kennedy. Boulder, CO: Westview Press, 1978.

Patterns of Japanese Policymaking: Experiences from Higher Education, by T. J. Pempel. Boulder, CO: Westview Press, 1978.

The Chinese Connection: Roger S. Greene, Thomas W. Lamont, George E. Sokolsky, and American-East Asian Relations, by Warren I. Cohen. New York: Columbia University Press, 1978.

Militarism in Modern China: The Career of Wu P'ei-fu, 1916–1939, by Odoric Y. K. Wou. Folkestone, England: Dawson, 1978.

A Chinese Pioneer Family: The Lins of Wu-Feng, by Johanna Meskill. Princeton University Press, 1979.

Perspectives on a Changing China, edited by Joshua A. Fogel and William T. Rowe. Boulder, CO: Westview Press, 1979.

The Memoirs of Li Tsung-jen, by T.K. Tong and Li Tsung-jen. Boulder, CO: Westview Press, 1979.

Unwelcome Muse: Chinese Literature in Shanghai and Peking, 1937–1945, by Edward Gunn. New York: Columbia University Press, 1979.

Yenan and the Great Powers: The Origins of Chinese Communist Foreign Policy, by James Reardon-Anderson. New York: Columbia University Press, 1980.

Uncertain Years: Chinese-American Relations, 1947–1950, edited by Dorothy Borg and Waldo Heinrichs. New York: Columbia University Press, 1980.

The Fateful Choice: Japan's Advance into Southeast Asia, edited by James William Morley. New York: Columbia University Press, 1980.

Tanaka Giichi and Japan's China Policy, by William F. Morton. Folkestone, England: Dawson, 1980; New York: St. Martin's

Press, 1980.

The Origins of the Korean War: Liberation and the Emergence of Separate Regimes, 1945-1947, by Bruce Cumings. Princeton: Princeton University Press, 1981.

Class Conflict in Chinese Socialism, by Richard Curt Kraus. New York: Columbia University Press, 1981.

Education Under Mao: Class and Competition in Canton Schools, by Jonathan Unger. New York: Columbia University Press, 1982.

Private Academies of Tokugawa Japan, by Richard Rubinger. Princeton: Princeton University Press, 1982.

Japan and the San Francisco Peace Settlement, by Michael M. Yoshitsu. New York: Columbia University Press, 1982.

New Frontiers in American-East Asian Relations: Essays Presented to Dorothy Borg, edited by Warren I. Cohen. New York: Columbia University Press, 1983.

The Origins of the Cultural Revolution: II, The Great Leap Forward, 1958-1960, by Roderick MacFarquhar. New York: Columbia University Press, 1983.

The China Quagmire: Japan's Expansion of the Asian Continent, 1933-1941, edited by James William Morley. New York: Columbia University Press, 1983.

Fragments of Rainbows: The Life and Poetry of Saito Mokichi, 1882-1953, by Amy Vladeck Heinrich. New York: Columbia University Press, 1983.

The U.S.-South Korean Alliance: Evolving Patterns of Security Relations, edited by Gerald L. Curtis and Sung-joo Han. Lexington, MA: Lexington Books, 1983.

Discovering History in China: American Historical Writing on the Recent Chinese Past, by Paul A. Cohen. New York: Columbia University Press, 1984.

The Foreign Policy of the Republic of Korea, edited by Youngnok Koo and Sungjoo Han. New York: Columbia University Press, 1984.

State and Diplomacy in Early Modern Japan, by Ronald Toby. Princeton: Princeton University Press, 1983 (hc); Stanford:

Stanford University Press, 1991 (pb).

Japan and the Asian Development Bank, by Dennis Yasutomo. New York: Praeger Publishers, 1983.

Japan Erupts: The London Naval Conference and the Manchurian Incident, edited by James W. Morley. New York: Columbia University Press, 1984.

Japanese Culture, third edition, revised, by Paul Varley. Honolulu: University of Hawaii Press, 1984.

The Foreign Policy of the Republic of Korea, edited by Youngnok Koo and Sung-joo Han. New York: Columbia University Press, 1985.

Japan's Modern Myths: Ideology in the Late Meiji Period, by Carol Gluck. Princeton: Princeton University Press, 1985.

Shamans, Housewives, and other Restless Spirits: Women in Korean Ritual Life, by Laurel Kendell. Honolulu: University of Hawaii Press, 1985.

Human Rights in Contemporary China, by R. Randle Edwards, Louis Henkin, and Andrew J. Nathan. New York: Columbia University Press, 1986.

The Pacific Basin: New Challenges for the United States, edited by James W. Morley. New York: Academy of Political Science, 1986.

The Manner of Giving: Strategic Aid and Japanese Foreign Policy, by Dennis T. Yasutomo. Lexington, MA: Lexington Books, 1986.

Security Interdependence in the Asia Pacific Region, James W. Morley, Ed., Lexington, MA: D.C. Heath and Co., 1986.

China's Political Economy: The Quest for Development since 1949, by Carl Riskin. Oxford: Oxford University Press, 1987.

Anvil of Victory: The Communist Revolution in Manchuria, by Steven I. Levine. New York: Columbia University Press, 1987.

Urban Japanese Housewives: At Home and in the Community, by Anne E. Imamura. Honolulu: University of Hawaii Press, 1987.

China's Satellite Parties, by James D. Seymour. Armonk, NY: M.E. Sharpe, 1987.

The Japanese Way of Politics, by Gerald L. Curtis. New York: Columbia University Press, 1988.

Border Crossings: Studies in International History, by Christopher Thorne. Oxford & New York: Basil Blackwell, 1988.

The Indochina Tangle: China's Vietnam Policy, 1975–1979, by Robert S. Ross. New York: Columbia University Press, 1988.

Remaking Japan: The American Occupation as New Deal, by Theodore Cohen, edited by Herbert Passin. New York: The Free Press, 1987.

Kim Il Sung: The North Korean Leader, by Dae-Sook Suh. New York: Columbia University Press, 1988.

Japan and the World, 1853–1952: A Bibliographic Guide to Recent Scholarship in Japanese Foreign Relations, by Sadao Asada. New York: Columbia University Press, 1988.

Contending Approaches to the Political Economy of Taiwan, edited by Edwin A. Winckler and Susan Greenhalgh. Armonk, NY: M.E. Sharpe, 1988.

Aftermath of War: Americans and the Remaking of Japan, 1945–1952, by Howard B. Schonberger. Kent, OH: Kent State University Press, 1989.

Single Sparks: China's Rural Revolutions, edited by Kathleen Hartford and Steven M. Goldstein. Armonk, NY: M.E. Sharpe, 1989.

Neighborhood Tokyo, by Theodore C. Bestor. Stanford: Stanford University Press, 1989.

Missionaries of the Revolution: Soviet Advisers and Chinese Nationalism, by C. Martin Wilbur Julie Lien-ying How. Cambridge, MA: Harvard University Press, 1989.

Education in Japan, by Richard Rubinger and Edward Beauchamp. New York: Garland Publishing, Inc., 1989.

Financial Politics in Contemporary Japan, by Frances Rosenbluth. Ithaca: Cornell University Press, 1989.

Suicidal Narrative in Modern Japan: The Case of Dazai Osamu, by Alan Wolfe. Princeton: Princeton University Press, 1990.

Thailand and the United States: Development, Security and Foreign

Aid, by Robert Muscat. New York: Columbia University Press, 1990.

Race to the Swift: State and Finance in Korean Industrialization, by Jung-En Woo. New York: Columbia University Press, 1990.

Anarchism and Chinese Political Culture, by Peter Zarrow. New York: Columbia University Press, 1990.

Competitive Ties: Subcontracting in the Japanese Automotive Industry, by Michael Smitka. New York: Columbia University Press, 1990.

China's Crisis: Dilemmas of Reform and Prospects for Democracy, by Andrew J. Nathan. Columbia University Press, 1990.

The Study of Change: Chemistry in China, 1840–1949, by James Reardon-Anderson. New York: Cambridge University Press, 1991.

Explaining Economic Policy Failure: Japan and the 1969–1971 International Monetary Crisis, by Robert Angel. New York: Columbia University Press, 1991.

Pacific Basin Industries in Distress: Structural Adjustment and Trade Policy in the Nine Industrialized Economies, edited by Hugh T. Patrick with Larry Meissner. New York: Columbia University Press, 1991.

Business Associations and the New Political Economy of Thailand: From Bureaucratic Polity to Liberal Corporatism, by Anek Laothamatas. Boulder, CO: Westview Press, 1991.

Constitutional Reform and the Future of the Republic of China, edited by Harvey J. Feldman. Armonk, NY: M.E. Sharpe, 1991.

Sowing Seeds of Change: Chinese Students, Japanese Teachers, 1895–1905, by Paula S. Harrell. Stanford: Stanford University Press, forthcoming.

Driven by Growth: Political Change in the Asia-Pacific Region, edited by James W. Morley. Armonk, NY: M. E. Sharpe, forthcoming.

Locality and State: Schoolhouse Politics During the Chinese Republic, by Helen Chauncey. Honolulu: University of Hawaii Press, forthcoming.

Social Mobility in Contemporary Japan, by Hiroshi Ishida. Stanford: Stanford University Press, forthcoming.

Pollution, Politics and Foreign Investment in Taiwan: The Lukang Rebellion, by James Reardon-Anderson. Armonk, NY: M. E. Sharpe, forthcoming.

Managing Indonesia: The Political Economy from 1965 to 1990, by John Bresnan. New York: Columbia University Press, forthcoming.

Tokyo's Marketplace, by Theodore C. Bestor. Stanford: Stanford University Press, forthcoming.

A graduate of Williams College, **James Reardon-Anderson** received his Ph.D. in political science from Columbia University. He has taught at the Chinese University of Hong Kong, the University of Michigan, and the Johns Hopkins University. Currently he is director of the Committee on Scholarly Communication with the People's Republic of China and Sun Yat-sen Professor of Chinese Studies at Georgetown University.

Professor Reardon-Anderson's publications include *Yenan and the Great Powers: The Origins of Chinese Communist Foreign Policy, 1944–46* (1980), *The Study of Change: Chemistry in China, 1840–1949* (1991), and *Grasslands and Grassland Science in Northern China* (forthcoming).

DATE

NOV 13 1986